Gary Chapman

NORTHFIELD PUBLISHING

CHICAGO

© 1992, 1995, 2004, 2010, 2015 by
Gary D. Chapman

All rights reserved. No part of this book may be reproduced in any form without permission in writing from the publisher, except in the case of brief quotations embodied in critical articles or reviews.

All Scripture quotations, unless otherwise indicated, are taken from the Holy Bible, New International Version®, NIV®. Copyright ©1973, 1978, 1984, 2011 by Biblica, Inc.™ Used by permission of Zondervan. All rights reserved worldwide. www.zondervan.com

Edited by Elizabeth Cody Newenhuyse
Cover design: Faceout Studio
Cover photo: Boone Rodriguez (boonerodriguez.com)
Author photo: P. S. Photography
Interior design: Smartt Guys design

Library of Congress Cataloging-in-Publication Data
Chapman, Gary D.
 The five love languages : the secret to love that lasts / Gary Chapman.
   p. cm.
 Includes bibliographical references.
 ISBN 978-0-8024-1270-6
 1. Marriage. 2. Communication in marriage. 3. Love. I. Title.
 HQ734.C4665 2010
 646.7'8—dc22
                                                           2009037112

We hope you enjoy this book from Northfield Publishing. Our goal is to provide high-quality, thought-provoking books and products that connect truth to your real needs and challenges. For more information on other books and products that will help you with all your important relationships, go to 5lovelanguages.com or write to:

Northfield Publishing
820 N. LaSalle Blvd.
Chicago, IL 60610

5 7 9 10 8 6

Printed in the United States of America

*To Karolyn,
Shelley, and Derek*

THE *5 love* LANGUAGES® Collection

The 5 Love Languages for Men

The 5 Love Languages Hardcover Special Edition

The 5 Love Languages of Children

The 5 Love Languages of Teenagers

The 5 Love Languages for Singles

The 5 Love Languages Military Edition

For more books by Gary Chapman,
go to 5lovelanguages.com

Contents

Acknowledgments		9
1.	What Happens to Love After the Wedding?	11
2.	Keeping the Love Tank Full	19
3.	Falling in Love	27
4.	Love Language #1: Words of Affirmation	37
5.	Love Language #2: Quality Time	55
6.	Love Language #3: Receiving Gifts	75
7.	Love Language #4: Acts of Service	91
8.	Love Language #5: Physical Touch	107
9.	Discovering Your Primary Love Language	119
10.	Love Is a Choice	131
11.	Love Makes the Difference	141
12.	Loving the Unlovely	149
13.	A Personal Word	165
	Frequently Asked Questions	171
	The 5 Love Languages Profile for Couples—for Him	191
	The 5 Love Languages Profile for Couples—for Her	197
	Notes	205

For a free online study guide please visit:

5lovelanguages.com

This group discussion guide is designed to both help couples apply the concepts from *The 5 Love Languages* and stimulate genuine dialogue among study groups.

Acknowledgments

Love begins, or should begin, at home. For me that means Sam and Grace, Dad and Mom. Without them I would still be seeking love instead of writing about it. Home also means Karolyn. If all wives loved as she does, fewer men would be looking over the fence. Shelley and Derek are now out of the nest, exploring new worlds, but I feel secure in the warmth of their love. I am blessed and grateful.

I am indebted to a host of professionals who have influenced my concepts of love. Among them are psychiatrists Ross Campbell and Judson Swihart. For editorial assistance, I am indebted to Debbie Barr, Cathy Peterson, and Betsey Newenhuyse. The technical expertise of Tricia Kube and Don Schmidt made it possible to meet publication deadlines. Last, and most important, I want to express my gratitude to the hundreds of couples who, over the years, have shared the intimate side of their lives with me. This book is a tribute to their honesty.

1

What Happens to Love After the Wedding?

At 30,000 feet, somewhere between Buffalo and Dallas, he put his magazine in his seat pocket, turned in my direction, and asked, "What kind of work do you do?"

"I do marriage counseling and lead marriage enrichment seminars," I said matter-of-factly.

"I've been wanting to ask someone this for a long time," he said. "What happens to the love after you get married?"

Relinquishing my hopes of getting a nap, I asked, "What do you mean?"

"Well," he said, "I've been married three times, and each time, it was wonderful before we got married, but somehow after the wedding it all fell apart. All the love I thought I had for her and the love she seemed to have for me evaporated. I am a fairly intelligent person. I operate a successful business, but I don't understand it."

"How long were you married?" I asked.

"The first one lasted about ten years. The second time, we were married three years, and the last one, almost six years."

"Did your love evaporate immediately after the wedding, or was it a gradual loss?" I inquired.

"Well, the second one went wrong from the very beginning. I don't know what happened. I really thought we loved each other, but the honeymoon was a disaster, and we never recovered. We only dated six months. It was a whirlwind romance. It was really exciting! But after the marriage, it was a battle from the beginning.

"In my first marriage, we had three or four good years before the baby came. After the baby was born, I felt like she gave her attention to the baby and I no longer mattered. It was as if her one goal in life was to have a baby, and after the baby, she no longer needed me."

"Did you tell her that?" I asked.

"Yes, I told her. She said I was crazy. She said I did not understand the stress of being a twenty-four-hour nurse. She said I should be more understanding and help her more. I really tried, but it didn't seem to make any difference. After that, we just grew further apart. After a while, there was no love left, just deadness. Both of us agreed that the marriage was over.

"My last marriage? I really thought that one would be different. I had been divorced for three years. We dated each other for two years. I really thought we knew what we were doing, and I thought that perhaps for the first time I really knew what it meant to love someone. I genuinely felt that she loved me.

"After the wedding, I don't think I changed. I continued to express love to her as I had before marriage. I told her how beautiful she was. I told her how much I loved her. I told her how proud I was to be her husband. But a few months after marriage, she started complaining;

about petty things at first—like my not taking the garbage out or not hanging up my clothes. Later, she went to attacking my character, telling me she didn't feel she could trust me, accusing me of not being faithful to her. She became a totally negative person. Before marriage, she was never negative. She was one of the most positive people I have ever met—that's one of the things that attracted me to her. She never complained about anything. Everything I did was wonderful, but once we were married, it seemed I could do nothing right. I honestly don't know what happened. Eventually, I lost my love for her and began to resent her. She obviously had no love for me. We agreed there was no benefit to our living together any longer, so we split.

"That was a year ago. So my question is, What happens to love after the wedding? Is my experience common? Is that why we have so many divorces in our country? I can't believe that it happened to me three times. And those who don't divorce, do they learn to live with the emptiness, or does love really stay alive in some marriages? If so, how?"

The questions my friend seated in 5A was asking are the questions that thousands of married and divorced persons are asking today. Some are asking friends, some are asking counselors and clergy, and some are asking themselves. Sometimes the answers are couched in psychological research jargon that is almost incomprehensible. Sometimes they are couched in humor and folklore. Most of the jokes and pithy sayings contain some truth, but they are like offering an aspirin to a person with cancer.

The desire for romantic love in marriage is deeply rooted in our

> **With all the help available from experts, why have so few couples found the secret to keeping love alive?**

psychological makeup. Books abound on the subject. Television and radio talk shows deal with it. The Internet is full of advice. So are our parents and friends and churches. Keeping love alive in our marriages is serious business.

With all the help available from media experts, why is it that so few couples seem to have found the secret to keeping love alive after the wedding? Why is it that a couple can attend a communication workshop, hear wonderful ideas on how to enhance communication, return home, and find themselves totally unable to implement the communication patterns demonstrated? How is it that we read something online on "101 Ways to Express Love to Your Spouse," select two or three ways that seem especially helpful, try them, and our spouse doesn't even acknowledge our effort? We give up on the other 98 ways and go back to life as usual.

THE TRUTH WE'RE MISSING

The answer to those questions is the purpose of this book. It is not that the books and articles already published are not helpful. The problem is that we have overlooked one fundamental truth: People speak different love languages.

My academic training is in the area of anthropology. Therefore, I have studied in the area of linguistics, which identifies a number of major language groups: Japanese, Chinese, Spanish, English, Portuguese, Arabic, Greek, German, French, and so on. Most of us grow up learning the language of our parents and siblings, which becomes our *primary* or native tongue. Later, we may learn additional languages—but usually with much more effort. These become our *secondary* languages. We speak and understand best our native language. We feel most comfortable speaking that language. The more we use a secondary language, the more comfortable we become conversing in it. If we speak only our primary language and encounter someone else who speaks only his or her primary language, which is different from ours, our communication will be limited. We must rely on pointing, grunting, drawing pictures, or acting out our ideas. We can communicate, but it is awkward. Language differences are part and parcel of human culture. If we are to communicate effectively across cultural lines, we must learn the language of those with whom we wish to communicate.

In the area of love, it is similar. Your emotional love language and the language of your spouse may be as different as Chinese from English. No matter how hard you try to express love in English, if your spouse understands only Chinese, you will never understand how to love each other. My friend on the plane was speaking the language of affirming words to his third wife when he said, "I told her how beautiful she was. I told her I loved her. I told her how proud I was to be her husband." He was speaking love, and he was sincere, but she did not understand his language. Perhaps she was looking for love in his behavior and didn't see it. Being sincere is not enough. We must be willing to learn our spouse's primary love language if we are to be effective communicators of love.

My conclusion after many years of marriage counseling is that there are five emotional love languages—five ways that people speak and understand emotional love. In the field of linguistics, a language may have numerous dialects or variations. Similarly, within the five basic emotional love languages, there are many dialects. The

The number of ways to express love within a love language is limited only by your imagination.

number of ways to express love within a love language is limited only by one's imagination. The important thing is to speak the love language of your spouse.

Seldom do a husband and wife have the same primary emotional love language. We tend to speak our primary love language, and we become confused when our spouse does not understand what we are communicating. We are expressing our love, but the message does not come through because we are speaking what, to them, is a foreign language. Therein lies the fundamental problem, and it is the purpose of this book to offer a solution. That is why I dare to write another book on love. Once we discover the five basic love languages and understand our own primary love language, as well as the primary love language of our spouse, we will then have the needed information to apply the ideas in the books and articles.

Once you identify and learn to speak your spouse's primary love language, I believe that you will have discovered the key to a long-lasting, loving marriage. Love need not evaporate after the wedding, but in order to keep it alive, most of us will have to put forth the effort to learn a secondary love language. We cannot rely on our native tongue if our spouse does not understand it. If we want them to feel the love we are trying to communicate, we must express it in their primary love language.

YOUR TURN

How does your spouse respond when you try to show affection?

2

Keeping the Love Tank Full

Love is the most important word in the English language—and the most confusing. Both secular and religious thinkers agree that love plays a central role in life. Love has a prominent role in thousands of books, songs, magazines, and movies. Numerous philosophical and theological systems have made a prominent place for love.

Psychologists have concluded that the need to feel loved is a primary human emotional need. For love, we will climb mountains, cross seas, traverse desert sands, and endure untold hardships. Without love, mountains become unclimbable, seas uncrossable, deserts unbearable, and hardship our lot in life.

If we can agree that the word *love* permeates human society, both historically and in the present, we must also agree that it is a most confusing word. We use it in a thousand ways. We say, "I love hot dogs," and in the next breath, "I love my mother." We speak of loving activities: swimming, skiing, hunting. We love objects: food, cars, houses.

We love animals: dogs, cats, even pet snails. We love nature: trees, grass, flowers, and weather. We love people: mother, father, son, daughter, parents, wives, husbands, friends. We even fall in love with love.

If all that is not confusing enough, we also use the word *love* to explain behavior. "I did it because I love her." That explanation is given for all kinds of actions. A politician is involved in an adulterous relationship, and he calls it love. The preacher, on the other hand, calls it sin. The wife of an alcoholic picks up the pieces after her husband's latest episode. She calls it love, but the psychologist calls it codependency. The parent indulges all the child's wishes, calling it love. The family therapist would call it irresponsible parenting. What is loving behavior?

The purpose of this book is not to eliminate all confusion surrounding the word *love* but to focus on that kind of love that is essential to our emotional health. Child psychologists affirm that every child has certain basic emotional needs that must be met if he is to be emotionally stable. Among those emotional needs, none is more basic than the need for love and affection, the need to sense that he or she belongs and is wanted. With an adequate supply of affection, the child will likely develop into a responsible adult. Without that love, he or she will be emotionally and socially challenged.

I liked the metaphor the first time I heard it: "Inside every child is an 'emotional tank' waiting to be filled with love. When a child really feels loved, he will develop normally, but when the love tank is empty, the child will misbehave. Much of the misbehavior of children is motivated by the cravings of an empty 'love tank.'" I was listening to Dr. Ross Campbell, a psychiatrist who specialized in the treatment of children and adolescents.

As I listened, I thought of the hundreds of parents who had

paraded the misdeeds of their children through my office. I had never visualized an empty love tank inside those children, but I had certainly seen the results of it. Their misbehavior was a misguided search for the love they did not feel. They were seeking love in all the wrong places and in all the wrong ways.

> **We needed love before we "fell in love," and we will need it as long as we live.**

I remember Ashley, who at thirteen years of age was being treated for a sexually transmitted disease. Her parents were crushed. They were angry with Ashley. They were upset with the school, which they blamed for teaching her about sex. "Why would she do this?" they asked.

In my conversation with Ashley, she told me of her parents' divorce when she was six years old. "I thought my father left because he didn't love me," she said. "When my mother remarried when I was ten, I felt she now had someone to love her, but I still had no one to love me. I wanted so much to be loved. I met this boy at school. He was older than me, but he liked me. I couldn't believe it. He was kind to me, and in a while I really felt he loved me. I didn't want to have sex, but I wanted to be loved."

Ashley's "love tank" had been empty for many years. Her mother and stepfather had provided for her physical needs but had not realized the deep emotional struggle raging inside her. They certainly loved Ashley, and they thought that she felt their love. Not until it was almost too late did they discover that they were not speaking Ashley's primary love language.

The emotional need for love, however, is not simply a childhood phenomenon. That need follows us into adulthood and into marriage. The "in-love" experience temporarily meets that need, but it is inevitably a quick fix and, as we shall learn later, has a limited and predictable life span. After we come down from the high of the "in-love" obsession, the emotional need for love resurfaces because it is fundamental to our nature. It is at the center of our emotional desires. We needed love before we "fell in love," and we will need it as long as we live.

The need to feel loved by one's spouse is at the heart of marital desires. A man said to me recently, "What good is the house, the cars, the place at the beach, or any of the rest of it if your wife doesn't love you?" Do you understand what he was really saying? "More than anything, I want to be loved by my wife." Material things are no replacement for human, emotional love. A wife says, "He ignores me all day long and then wants to jump in bed with me. I hate it." She is not a wife who hates sex; she is a wife desperately pleading for emotional love.

OUR CRY FOR LOVE

Something in our nature cries out to be loved by another. Isolation is devastating to the human psyche. That is why solitary confinement is considered the cruelest of punishments. At the heart of humankind's existence is the desire to be intimate and to be loved by another. Marriage is designed to meet that need for intimacy and love. That is why the ancient biblical writings spoke of the husband and wife becoming "one flesh." That did not mean that individuals would lose their identity; it meant that they would enter into each other's lives in a deep and intimate way.

But if love is important, it is also elusive. I have listened to many married couples share their secret pain. Some came to me because the inner ache had become unbearable. Others came because they realized that their behavior patterns or the misbehavior of their spouse was destroying the marriage. Some came simply to inform me that they no longer wanted to be married. Their dreams of "living happily ever after" had been dashed against the hard walls of reality. Again and again I have heard the words "Our love is gone; our relationship is dead. We used to feel close, but not now. We no longer enjoy being with each other. We don't meet each other's needs." Their stories bear testimony that adults as well as children have "love tanks."

Could it be that deep inside hurting couples exists an invisible "emotional love tank" with its gauge on empty? Could the misbehavior, withdrawal, harsh words, and critical spirit occur because of that empty tank? If we could find a way to fill it, could the marriage be reborn? With a full tank would couples be able to create an emotional climate where it is possible to discuss differences and resolve conflicts? Could that tank be the key that makes marriage work?

Those questions sent me on a long journey. Along the way, I discovered the simple yet powerful insights contained in this book. The journey has taken me not only through years of marriage counseling but into the hearts and minds of hundreds of couples throughout America. From Seattle to Miami, couples have invited me into the inner chamber of their marriages, and we have talked openly. The illustrations included in this book are cut from the fabric of real life. Only names and places are changed to protect the privacy of the individuals who have spoken so freely.

I am convinced that keeping the emotional love tank full is as important to a marriage as maintaining the proper oil level is to an automobile. Running your marriage on an empty "love tank"

> **Whatever the quality of your marriage now, it can always be better.**

may cost you even more than trying to drive your car without oil. What you are about to read has the potential of saving thousands of marriages and can even enhance the emotional climate of a good marriage. Whatever the quality of your marriage now, it can always be better.

> **WARNING:** Understanding the five love languages and learning to speak the primary love language of your spouse may radically affect his or her behavior. People behave differently when their emotional love tanks are full.

Before we examine the five love languages, however, we must address one other important but confusing phenomenon: the euphoric experience of "falling in love."

YOUR TURN

On a scale of 0–10, how full is your love tank?

3

Falling in Love

She showed up at my office without an appointment and asked my assistant if she could see me for five minutes. I had known Rachel for eighteen years. She was thirty-six and had never married. From time to time, she had made appointments with me to discuss a particular difficulty in one of her dating relationships. She was by nature a conscientious, caring person, so it was completely out of character for her to show up at my office unannounced. I thought, *There must be some terrible crisis for Rachel to come without an appointment.* I told my assistant to show her in, and I fully expected to see her burst into tears and tell me some tragic story as soon as the door was closed. Instead, she practically skipped into my office, beaming with excitement.

"How are you today, Rachel?" I asked.

"Great!" she said. "I've never been better in my life. I'm getting married!"

"You *are*?" I said. "To whom and when?"

"His name is Ben," she said. "We're getting married in September."

"That's exciting. How long have you been dating?"

"Three weeks. I know it's crazy, Dr. Chapman, after all the people I have dated and the number of times I came so close to getting married. I can't believe it myself, but I know Ben is the one for me. From the first date, we both knew it. Of course, we didn't talk about it on the first night, but one week later, he asked me to marry him. I knew he was going to ask me, and I knew I was going to say yes. I have never felt this way before. You know about the relationships that I have had through the years and the struggles I have had. In every relationship, something was not right. I never felt at peace about marrying any of them, but I know that Ben is the right one."

By this time, Rachel was rocking back and forth in her chair, giggling and saying, "I know it's crazy, but I am so happy. I have never been this happy in my life."

What has happened to Rachel? She has fallen in love. In her mind, Ben is the most wonderful man she has ever met. He is perfect in every way. He will make the ideal husband. She thinks about him day and night. The facts that Ben has been married twice before, has three children, and has had three jobs in the past year are trivial to Rachel. She's happy, and she is convinced that she is going to be happy forever with Ben. She is in love.

> We have been led to believe that if we are really in love, it will last forever.

Most of us enter marriage by way of the "in-love" experience. We meet someone whose physical characteristics and personality traits create enough electrical shock to trigger our "love alert" system. The bells go off, and we set in motion the process of getting to know the person. The first step may be sharing a hamburger or steak, depending on our budget, but our real interest is not in the food. We are on a quest to discover love. "Could this warm, tingly feeling I have inside be the 'real' thing?"

Sometimes we lose the tingles on the first date. We find out that he spends time on crackpot websites or she attended six colleges, and the tingles run right out our toes; we want no more hamburgers with them. Other times, however, the tingles are stronger after the burger than before. We arrange for a few more "together" experiences, and before long the level of intensity has increased to the point where we find ourselves saying, "I think I'm falling in love." Eventually we are convinced that it is the "real thing," and we tell the other person, hoping the feeling is reciprocal. If it isn't, things cool off a bit or we redouble our efforts to impress, and eventually win the love of, our beloved. When it is reciprocal, we start talking about marriage because everyone agrees that being "in love" is the necessary foundation for a good marriage.

THE ANTEROOM OF HEAVEN

At its peak, the "in-love" experience is euphoric. We are emotionally obsessed with each other. We go to sleep thinking of one another. When we rise, that person is the first thought on our minds. We long to be together. Spending time together is like playing in the anteroom of heaven. When we hold hands, it seems as if our blood flows together. We could kiss forever if we didn't have to go to school or work. When we embrace, time seems to stop . . .

The person who is "in love"—we'll call her Jen—has the illusion that her beloved is perfect. Her best friend can see the flaws—it bothers her how he talks to Jen sometimes—but Jen won't listen. Her mother, noting the young man seems unable to hold a steady job, keeps her concerns to herself but asks polite questions about "Ryan's plans."

Our dreams before marriage are of marital bliss: "We are going to make each other supremely happy. Other couples may argue and fight, but not us. We love each other." Of course, we are not totally naive. We know intellectually that we will eventually have differences. But we are certain that we will discuss those differences openly; one of us will always be willing to make concessions, and we will reach agreement. It's hard to believe anything else when you are in love.

We have been led to believe that if we are really in love, it will last forever. We will always have the wonderful feelings that we have at this moment. Nothing could ever come between us. Nothing will ever overcome our love for each other. We are caught up in the beauty and charm of the other's personality. Our love is the most wonderful thing we have ever experienced. We observe that some married couples seem to have lost that feeling, but it will never happen to us. "Maybe they didn't have the real thing," we reason.

Unfortunately, the eternality of the "in-love" experience is fiction, not fact. The late psychologist Dr. Dorothy Tennov conducted long-range studies on the in-love phenomenon. After studying scores of couples, she concluded that the average life span of a romantic obsession is two years. If it is a secretive love affair, it may last a little longer. Eventually, however, we all descend from the clouds and plant our feet on earth again. Our eyes are opened, and we see the warts of the other person. Her endearing "quirks" are now merely annoying. His sharp sense of humor now wounds. Those little bumps we overlooked when we were in love now become huge mountains.

REALITY INTRUDES

Welcome to the real world of marriage, where hairs are always on the sink and little white spots cover the mirror, where discussions center not on "where should we eat tonight?" but "why didn't you get milk?" It is a world where bills and in-laws and jobs and children all clamor for our attention, a world where routine and resentment can silently eat away at the love we once had. In this world, a look can hurt and a word can crush. Intimate lovers can become enemies, and marriage a battlefield.

What happened to the "in-love" experience? Alas, it was but an illusion by which we were tricked into signing our names on the dotted line, for better or for worse. No wonder so many have come to curse marriage and the partner whom they once loved. After all, if we were deceived, we have a right to be angry. Did we really have the "real" thing? I think so. The problem was faulty information.

The bad information was the idea that the "in-love" obsession would last forever. We should have known better. A casual observation should have taught us that if people remained obsessed, we would all be in serious trouble. The shock waves would rumble through business, industry, church, education, and the rest of society. Why? Because people who are "in love" lose interest in other pursuits. That is why we call it "obsession." The college student who falls head over heels in love sees his grades tumbling. It is difficult to study when you are in love. Tomorrow you have a test on the War of 1812, but who cares about the War of 1812? When you're in love, everything else seems irrelevant. A man said to me, "Dr. Chapman, my job is disintegrating."

"What do you mean?" I asked.

> **We fail to reckon with the reality of human nature.**

"I met this girl, fell in love, and I can't get a thing done. I can't keep my mind on my job. I spend my day dreaming about her."

The euphoria of the "in-love" state gives us the illusion that we have an intimate relationship. We feel that we belong to each other. We believe we can conquer all problems. We feel altruistic toward each other. As one young man said about his fiancée, "I can't conceive of doing anything to hurt her. My only desire is to make her happy. I would do anything to make her happy." Such obsession gives us the false sense that our egocentric attitudes have been eradicated and we have become sort of a Mother Teresa, willing to give anything for the benefit of our lover. The reason we can do that so freely is that we sincerely believe that our lover feels the same way toward us. We believe that she is committed to meeting our needs, that he loves us as much as we love him and would never do anything to hurt us.

That thinking is always fanciful. Not that we are insincere in what we think and feel, but we are unrealistic. We fail to reckon with the reality of human nature. By nature, we are egocentric. Our world revolves around us. None of us is totally altruistic. The euphoria of the "in-love" experience only gives us that illusion.

Once the experience of falling in love has run its natural course (remember, the average in-love experience lasts two years), we will return to the world of reality and begin to assert ourselves. He will express his desires, but his desires will be different from hers. He wants sex, but she is too tired. He dreams of buying a new car, but she flatly says, "We can't afford it." She would like to visit her parents, but he says, "I don't like spending so much time with your family." Little by little, the illusion of intimacy evaporates, and the individual desires, emotions, thoughts, and behavior patterns assert themselves. They are two individuals. Their minds have not melded together, and their emotions mingled only briefly in the ocean of love. Now the waves of reality begin to separate them. They fall out of love, and at that point either they withdraw, separate, divorce, and set off in search of a new in-love experience, or they begin the hard work of learning to love each other without the euphoria of the in-love obsession.

Some couples believe that the end of the "in-love" experience means they have only two options: resign themselves to a life of misery with their spouse; or jump ship and try again. Our generation has opted for the latter, whereas an earlier generation often chose the former. Before we automatically conclude that we have made the better choice, perhaps we should examine the data. The divorce rate for second marriages is higher than the divorce rate of first marriages. The divorce rate in third marriages is higher still. Apparently the prospect of a happier marriage the second and third time around is not substantial.

> **I need to be loved by someone who chooses to love me.**

FROM "IN LOVE" TO REAL LOVE

Research seems to indicate that there is a third and better alternative: We can recognize the in-love experience for what it was—a temporary emotional high—and now pursue "real love" with our spouse. That kind of love is emotional in nature but not obsessional. It is a love that unites reason and emotion. It involves an act of the will and requires discipline, and it recognizes the need for personal growth. Our most basic emotional need is not to fall in love but to be genuinely loved by another, to know a love that grows out of reason and choice, not instinct. I need to be loved by someone who chooses to love me, who sees in me something worth loving.

That kind of love requires effort and discipline. It is the choice to expend energy in an effort to benefit the other person, knowing that if his or her life is enriched by your effort, you too will find a sense of satisfaction—the satisfaction of having genuinely loved another. It does not require the euphoria of the "in-love" experience. In fact, true love cannot begin until the "in-love" experience has run its course.

We cannot take credit for the kind and generous things we do while under the influence of "the obsession." We are pushed and carried along by an instinctual force that goes beyond our normal behavior patterns. But if, once we return to the real world of human choice, we choose to be kind and generous, that is real love.

The emotional need for love must be met if we are to have emotional health. Married adults long to feel affection and love from their spouses. We feel secure when we are assured that our mate accepts us, wants us, and is committed to our well-being. During the "in-love" stage, we felt all of those emotions. It was heavenly while it lasted. Our mistake was in thinking it would last forever.

But that obsession was not meant to last forever. In the textbook of marriage, it is but the introduction. The heart of the book is rational, volitional love. That is the kind of love to which the sages have always called us. It is intentional.

That is good news to the married couple who have lost all of their "in-love" feelings. If love is a choice, then they have the capacity to love after the "in-love" obsession has died and they have returned to the real world. That kind of love begins with an attitude—a way of thinking. Love is the attitude that says, "I am married to you, and I choose to look out for your interests." Then the one who chooses to love will find appropriate ways to express that decision.

"But it seems so sterile," some may contend. "Love as an attitude with appropriate behavior? Where are the shooting stars, the balloons, the deep emotions? What about the spirit of anticipation, the twinkle of the eye, the electricity of a kiss, the excitement of sex? What about the emotional security of knowing that I am number one in his/her mind?" That is what this book is all about. How do we meet each other's deep, emotional need to feel loved? If we can learn that and choose to do it, then the love we share will be exciting beyond anything we ever felt when we were infatuated.

For many years now, I have discussed the five emotional love languages in my marriage seminars and in private counseling sessions. Thousands of couples will attest to the validity of what you are about to read. My files are filled with letters from people whom I have never met, saying, "A friend loaned me one of your DVDs on love languages, and it has revolutionized our marriage. We had struggled for years trying to love each other, but our efforts had missed each other emotionally. Now that we are speaking the appropriate love languages, the emotional climate of our marriage has radically improved."

When your spouse's emotional love tank is full and he feels secure in your love, the whole world looks bright and your spouse will move out to reach his highest potential in life. But when the love tank is empty and he feels used but not loved, the whole world looks dark and he will likely never reach his potential for good in the world. In the next five chapters, I will explain the five emotional love languages and then, in chapter 9, illustrate how discovering your spouse's primary love language can make your efforts at love most productive.

YOUR TURN

Can you pinpoint a time in your marriage when "reality" set in? How did this affect your relationship, for better or worse?

4

Love Language #1
Words of Affirmation

Mark Twain once said, "I can live for two months on a good compliment." If we take Twain literally, six compliments a year would have kept his emotional love tank at the operational level. Your spouse will probably need more.

One way to express love emotionally is to use words that build up. Solomon, author of the ancient Hebrew Wisdom Literature, wrote, "The tongue has the power of life and death."[1] Many couples have never learned the tremendous power of verbally affirming each other.

Verbal compliments, or words of appreciation, are powerful communicators of love. They are best expressed in simple, straightforward statements of affirmation, such as:

"You look sharp in that suit."

"Do you ever look incredible in that dress! Wow!"

"I really like how you're always on time to pick me up at work."

"Thanks for getting the babysitter lined up tonight. I want you to know I don't take that for granted."

"You can always make me laugh."

What would happen to the emotional climate of a marriage if the husband and wife heard such words of affirmation regularly?

Several years ago, I was sitting in my office with my door open. A lady walking down the hall said, "Have you got a minute?"

"Sure, come in."

She sat down and said, "Dr. Chapman, I've got a problem. I can't get my husband to paint our bedroom. I have been after him for nine months. I have tried everything I know, and I can't get him to paint it."

My first thought was, *Lady, you are at the wrong place. I am not a paint contractor.* But I said, "Tell me about it."

She said, "Well, last Saturday was a good example. You remember how pretty it was? Do you know what my husband did all day long? He was cleaning out his computer files."

"So what did you do?"

"I went in there and said, 'Dan, I don't understand you. Today would have been a perfect day to paint the bedroom, and here you are working on your computer.'"

"So did he paint the bedroom?" I inquired.

"No. It's still not painted. I don't know what to do."

"Let me ask you a question," I said. "Are you opposed to computers?"

"No, but I want the bedroom painted."

"Are you certain that your husband knows that you want the bedroom painted?"

"I know he does," she said. "I have been after him for nine months."

"Let me ask you one more question. Does your husband ever do anything good?"

"Like what?"

"Oh, like taking the garbage out, or putting gas in the car, or paying the electric bill, or running to the store to get milk and toilet paper?"

"Yes," she said, "he does some of those things."

"Then I have two suggestions. One, don't ever mention painting the bedroom again." I repeated, "Don't ever mention it again."

"I don't see how that's going to help," she said.

"Look, you just told me that he knows that you want the bedroom painted. You don't have to tell him anymore. He already knows. The second suggestion I have is that the next time your husband does anything good, give him a verbal compliment. If he takes the garbage out, say, 'Dan, I want you to know that I really appreciate your taking the garbage out.' Don't say, 'About time you took the garbage out. The flies were going to carry it out for you.' If you see him paying the electric bill, put your hand on his shoulder and say, 'Dan, I really appreciate your paying the electric bill. I hear there are husbands who don't do that, and I want you to know how much I appreciate it.' Or, 'I really appreciated you running out to the store when I had to finish that project.' Every time he does anything good, give him a verbal compliment."

Verbal compliments are far greater motivators than nagging words.

"I don't see how that's going to get the bedroom painted."

I said, "You asked for my advice. You have it. It's free."

She wasn't very happy with me when she left. Three weeks later, however, she came back to my office and said, "It worked!" She had learned that verbal compliments are far greater motivators than nagging words.

I am not suggesting verbal flattery in order to get your spouse to do something you want. The object of love is not getting something you want but doing something for the well-being of the one you love. It is a fact, however, that when we receive affirming words we are far more likely to be motivated to reciprocate and do something our spouse desires.

ENCOURAGING WORDS

Giving verbal compliments is only one way to express words of affirmation to your spouse. Another dialect is encouraging words. The word *encourage* means "to inspire courage." All of us have areas in which we feel insecure. We lack courage, and that lack of courage often hinders us from accomplishing the positive things that we would like to do. The latent potential within your spouse in his or her areas of insecurity may await your encouraging words.

Allison had always liked to write. Late in her college career, she took a few courses in journalism. She quickly realized that her excitement about writing exceeded her interest in history, which had been her academic major. It was too late to change majors, but after college and especially before the first baby, she wrote several articles. She submitted one article to a magazine, but when she received a rejection slip, she never had the courage to submit another. Now that the children were older and she had more time to contemplate, Allison was again writing.

Keith, Allison's husband, had paid little attention to Allison's writing in the early days of their marriage. He was busy with his own profession and trying to make a place for himself in that world. In time, however, Keith had realized that life's deepest meaning is not found in accomplishments but in relationships. He had learned to give more attention to Allison and her interests. So it was quite natural one night for him to pick up one of Allison's articles and read it. When he finished, he went into the den where Allison was reading a book. With great enthusiasm, he said, "I hate to interrupt your reading, but I have to tell you this. I just finished reading your article on 'Making the Most of the Holidays.' Allison, you're a really good writer. This stuff ought to be published! You write clearly. Your words paint pictures that I can visualize. You have great ideas. You have to submit this to some magazines."

"Do you really think so?" Allison asked hesitantly.

"I know so," Keith said. "I'm telling you, this is good."

When Keith left the room, Allison did not resume her reading. With the closed book in her lap, she dreamed for thirty minutes about what Keith had said. She wondered if others would view her writing the same way he did. She remembered the rejection slip she had received years ago, but she reasoned that she was a different person now. Her writing was better. She had had more experiences. Before she left the chair to get a drink of water, Allison had made a decision. She would submit her articles to some magazines. She would see if they could be published.

Keith's encouraging words were spoken many years ago. Allison has had numerous articles published since then and now has a book contract. She is an excellent writer, but it took the encouraging words from her husband to inspire her to take the first step in the arduous process of getting an article published.

Perhaps your spouse has untapped potential in one or more areas of life. That potential may be awaiting your encouraging words. Perhaps she needs to enroll in a course to develop that potential. Maybe he needs to meet some people who have succeeded in that area, who can give him insight on the next step he needs to take. Your words may give your spouse the courage necessary to take that first step.

Please note that I am not talking about pressuring your spouse to do something that *you* want. I am talking about encouraging him to develop an interest that he already has. For example, a wife might pressure her husband to look for a more lucrative job. The wife thinks she's encouraging her spouse, but to him it sounds more like condemnation. But if he has the desire and motivation to seek a better position, her words will bolster his resolve. Until he has that desire, her words will come across as judgmental and guilt inducing. They express not love but rejection.

> **Encouragement requires empathy and seeing the world from your spouse's perspective.**

If, however, he says, "You know, I've been thinking about starting a handyman business on the side," then she has an opportunity to give words of encouragement. Encouraging words would sound like this. "If you decide to do that, I can tell you one thing. You will be a success. That's one of the things I like about you. When you set your mind to something, you do it. If that's what you want to do, I will certainly do everything I can to help you." Such words may give him the courage to start drawing up a list of potential clients.

Encouragement requires empathy and seeing the world from your spouse's perspective. We must first learn what is important to our spouse. Only then can we give encouragement. With verbal encouragement, we are trying to communicate, "I know. I care. I am with you. How can I help?" We are trying to show that we believe in him and in his abilities. We are giving credit and praise.

Most of us have more potential than we will ever develop. What holds us back is often courage. A loving spouse can supply that all-important catalyst. Of course, encouraging words may be difficult for you to speak. It may not be your primary love language. If you have a pattern of critical and condemning words it may take great effort for you to learn this second language, but I can assure you that it will be worth the effort.

KIND WORDS

Love is kind. If then we are to communicate love verbally, we must use kind words. That has to do with the way we speak. The same sentence can have two different meanings, depending on how you say it. The statement "I love you," when said with kindness and tenderness, can be a genuine expression of love. But what about "I love you?" The question mark changes the whole meaning of those three words. Sometimes our words say one thing, but our tone of voice says another. We are sending double messages. Our spouse will usually interpret our message based on our tone of voice, not the words we use.

"I would be delighted to wash dishes tonight," said in a snarling tone will not be received as an expression of love. On the other hand, we can share pain, sadness, and even anger in a kind manner, and that will be an expression of love. "I felt disappointed and hurt that you didn't offer to help me this evening," said with gentle directness, can be an expression of love. The person speaking wants to be known by her spouse. She is taking steps to build intimacy by sharing her feelings. She is asking for an opportunity to discuss a hurt in order to find healing. The same words expressed with a loud, harsh voice will be not an expression of love but an expression of condemnation and judgment.

The manner in which we speak is exceedingly important. An ancient sage once said, "A soft answer turns away anger." When your spouse is angry and upset and lashing out words of heat, if you choose to be loving, you will not reciprocate with additional heat but with a soft voice. You will receive what he is saying as information about his emotional feelings. You will let him tell you of his hurt, anger, and perception of events. You will seek to put yourself in his shoes and see the event through his eyes and then express softly and kindly your understanding of why he feels that way. If you have wronged him, you will be willing to confess the wrong and ask forgiveness. If your motivation is different from what he is reading, you will be able to explain your motivation kindly. You will seek understanding and reconciliation, and not to prove your own perception as the only logical way to interpret what has happened. That is mature love—love to which we aspire if we seek a growing marriage.

> **Forgiveness is the way of love.**

Love doesn't keep a score of wrongs. Love doesn't bring up past failures. None of us is perfect. In marriage we do not always do the best or right thing. We have sometimes done and said hurtful things to our spouses. We cannot erase the past. We can only confess it and agree that it was wrong. We can ask for forgiveness and try to act differently in the future. Having confessed my failure and asked forgiveness, I can do nothing more to mitigate the hurt it may have caused my spouse. When I have been wronged by my spouse and she has painfully confessed it and requested forgiveness, I have the option of justice or forgiveness. If I choose justice and seek to pay her back or make her pay for her wrongdoing, I am making myself the judge and she the felon. Intimacy becomes impossible. If, however, I choose to forgive, intimacy can be restored. Forgiveness is the way of love.

I am amazed by how many individuals mess up every new day with yesterday. They insist on bringing into today the failures of yesterday, and in so doing, they pollute a potentially wonderful present. "I can't believe you did it. I don't think I'll ever forget it. You can't possibly know how much you hurt me. I don't know how you can sit there so smugly after you treated me that way. You ought to be crawling on your knees, begging me for forgiveness. I don't know if I can ever forgive you." Those are not the words of love but of bitterness and resentment and revenge.

The best thing we can do with the failures of the past is to let them be history. Yes, it happened. Certainly it hurt. And it may still hurt, but he has acknowledged his failure and asked your forgiveness. We cannot erase the past, but we can accept it as history. We can choose to live today free from the failures of yesterday. Forgiveness is not a feeling; it is a commitment. It is a choice to show mercy, not to hold the offense up against the offender. Forgiveness is an expression of love. "I love you. I care about you, and I choose to forgive you. Even though my feelings of hurt may linger, I will not allow what has happened to come between us. I hope that we can learn from this experience. You are not a failure because you have failed. You are my spouse, and together we will go on from here." Those are the words of affirmation expressed in the dialect of kind words.

HUMBLE WORDS

Love makes requests, not demands. When I demand things from my spouse, I become a parent and she the child. It is the parent who tells the three-year-old what he ought to do and, in fact, what he must do.

That is necessary because the three-year-old does not yet know how to navigate in the treacherous waters of life. In marriage, however, we are equal, adult partners. We are not perfect to be sure, but we are adults and we are partners. If we are to develop an intimate relationship, we need to know each other's desires. If we wish to love each other, we need to know what the other person wants.

The way we express those desires, however, is all-important. If they come across as demands, we have erased the possibility of intimacy and will drive our spouse away. If, however, we make our needs and desires known in the form of a request, we are giving guidance, not ultimatums. The husband who says, "Could you make that good pasta one of these nights?" is giving his wife guidance on how to love him and thus build intimacy. On the other hand, the husband who says, "Can't we ever have a decent meal around here?" is being whiny, is making a demand, and his wife is likely to fire back, "Okay, you cook!" The wife who says, "Do you think it will be possible for you to clean the gutters this weekend?" is expressing love by making a request. But the wife who says, "If you don't get those gutters cleaned out soon, they are going to fall off the house. They already have trees growing out of them!" has ceased to love and has become a domineering spouse.

When you make a request of your spouse, you are affirming his or her worth and abilities. You are in essence indicating that she has something or can do something that is meaningful and worthwhile to you. When, however, you make demands, you have become not a lover but a tyrant. Your spouse will feel not affirmed but belittled. A request introduces the element of choice. Your mate may choose to respond to your request or to deny it, because love is always a choice. That's what makes it meaningful. To know that my spouse loves me enough to respond to one of my requests communicates emotionally that she cares about me, respects me, admires me, and wants to do something to please me.

We cannot get emotional love by way of demand. My spouse may in fact comply with my demands, but it is not an expression of love. It is an act of fear or guilt or some other emotion, but not love. Thus, a request creates the possibility for an expression of love, whereas a demand suffocates that possibility.

NOTEBOOKS—AND MORE

Words of affirmation are one of the five basic love languages. Within that language, however, there are many dialects. We have discussed a few already, and there are many more. Entire volumes and numerous articles have been written on these dialects. All of the dialects have in common the use of words to affirm one's spouse. Psychologist William James said that possibly the deepest human need is the need to feel appreciated. Words of affirmation will meet that need in many individuals. If you are not a man or woman of words, if it is not your primary love language but you think it may be the love language of your spouse, let me suggest that you keep a notebook titled "Words of Affirmation." When you read an article or book on love, record the words of affirmation you find. When you hear a lecture on love or you overhear a friend saying something positive about another person, write it down. In time, you will collect quite a list of words to use in communicating love to your spouse.

You may also want to try giving indirect words of affirmation—that is, saying positive things about your spouse when he or she is not present. Eventually, someone will tell your spouse, and you will get full credit for love. Tell your wife's mother how great your wife is. When her mother tells her what you said, it will be amplified, and you will get even more credit. Also affirm your spouse in front of others when he or she is present. When you are given public honor for an accomplishment, be sure to share the credit with your spouse. You may also try your hand at writing words of affirmation. Written words have the benefit of being read over and over again.

I learned an important lesson about words of affirmation and love languages years ago in Little Rock, Arkansas, when I visited Mark and Andrea in their home on a beautiful spring day. The setting was idyllic—on the outside. Once inside, however, I discovered the truth. Their marriage was in shambles. Twelve years and two children after the wedding day, they wondered why they had married in the first place. They seemed to disagree on everything. The only thing they really agreed on was that they both loved the children.

As the story unfolded, my observation was that Mark was a workaholic who had little time left over for Andrea. Andrea worked part-time, mainly to get out of the house. Their method of coping was withdrawal. They tried to put distance between themselves so that their conflicts would not seem as large. But the gauge on both love tanks read "empty."

They told me that they had been going for marriage counseling but didn't seem to be making much progress. They were attending my marriage seminar, and I was leaving town the next day. This would likely be my only encounter with them, so I decided to put everything on the table.

I spent an hour with each of them separately. I listened intently to both stories. I discovered that in spite of the emptiness of their relationship and their many disagreements, they appreciated certain things about each other. Mark acknowledged Andrea was a "good mother." But, he continued, "there is simply no affection coming from her. I work my tail off and she doesn't appreciate it." In my conversation with Andrea, she agreed that Mark was an excellent provider. "But," she complained, "he does nothing around the house to help me, and he never has time for me. What's the use of having nice things if you don't ever get to enjoy them together?"

With that information, I decided to focus my advice by making only one suggestion to each of them. I told Mark and Andrea separately that each one held the key to changing the emotional climate of the marriage. "That key," I said, "is to express verbal appreciation for the things you like about the other person and, for the moment, suspending your complaints about the things you do not like." We reviewed the positive comments they had already made about each other, and I helped each of them write a list of those positive traits. Mark's list focused on Andrea's activities with her children, home, and church. Andrea's list focused on Mark's hard work and financial provision of the family. We made the lists as specific as possible. Andrea's list looked like this:

- He is aggressive in his work.
- He has received several promotions through the years.
- He's a good financial manager.
- He is always thinking of ways to improve his productivity.
- He's generous with finances and agrees I can use the money from my job any way I desire.

Mark's list looked like this:
- She keeps our house clean and orderly.
- She helps the kids with their homework.
- She cooks dinner about three days a week.
- She teaches first-grade Sunday school.
- She chauffeurs the children to all their activities.

I suggested that they add to the lists things they noticed in the weeks ahead. I also suggested that twice a week, they select one positive trait and express verbal appreciation for it to the spouse. I gave one further guideline. I told Andrea that if Mark happened to give her a compliment, she was not to give him a compliment at the same time, but rather, she should simply receive it and say, "Thank you for saying that." I told Mark the same thing. I encouraged them to do that every week for two months, and if they found it helpful, they could continue. If the experiment did not help the emotional climate of the marriage, then they could write it off as another failed attempt.

The next day, I got on the plane and returned home. I made a note to follow up with them two months later to see what had happened. When I called them in midsummer, I asked to speak to each of them individually. I was amazed to find that Mark's attitude had taken a giant step forward. He had guessed that I had given Andrea the same advice I had given him, but that was all right. He loved it. She was expressing appreciation for his hard work and his provision for the family. "She has actually made me feel like a man again. We've got a ways to go, Dr. Chapman, but I really believe we are on the road."

When I talked to Andrea, however, I found that she had only taken a baby step forward. She said, "It has improved some, Dr. Chapman. Mark is giving me verbal compliments as you suggested, and I guess he is sincere. But he's still not spending any time with me. He is still so busy at work that we never have time together."

As I listened to Andrea, I knew that I had made a significant discovery. The love language of one person is not necessarily the love language of another. It was obvious that Mark's primary love language was words of affirmation. He was a hard worker, and he enjoyed his work, but what he wanted most from his wife was expressions of appreciation for his work. That pattern was probably set in childhood, and the need for verbal affirmation was no less important in his adult life. Andrea, on the other hand, was emotionally crying out for something else. That brings us to love language number two.

YOUR TURN

What would you most like to hear your spouse say to you?

IF YOUR SPOUSE'S LOVE LANGUAGE IS
WORDS OF AFFIRMATION:

1. To remind yourself that "Words of Affirmation" is your spouse's primary love language, print the following on a card and put it on a mirror or other place where you will see it daily:

   Words are important!

   Words are important!

   Words are important!

2. For one week, keep a written record of all the words of affirmation you give your spouse each day. You might be surprised how well (or how poorly) you are speaking words of affirmation.

3. Set a goal to give your spouse a different compliment each day for one month. If "an apple a day keeps the doctor away," maybe a compliment a day will keep the counselor away. (You may want to record these compliments also, so you will not duplicate the statements.)

4. Learn to say "I love you" or other expressions of affirmation in a couple of different languages.

5. Compliment your spouse in the presence of his parents or friends. You will get double credit: Your spouse will feel loved and the parents will feel lucky to have such a great son-in-law or daughter-in-law.

6. Look for your spouse's strengths and tell her how much you appreciate those strengths. Be specific: "I like how you reach out to people at church who don't seem to have anyone to talk to." Or: "You're really keeping up with the job search. I know it'll pay off."

7. Occasionally email or text a note of affirmation during the day or when one of you is traveling. Or if you know your spouse is having a hard day, send a link to a funny website.

8. Thank your mate for something they do routinely and wouldn't expect to be complimented for.

QUALITY TIME

5

LOVE LANGUAGE #2

Quality Time

I should have picked up on Andrea's primary love language from the beginning. What was she saying on that spring night when I visited her and Mark in Little Rock? "Mark doesn't spend any time with me. What good are all our things if we don't ever enjoy them together?" What was her desire? Quality time with Mark. She wanted his attention. She wanted him to focus on her, to give her time, to do things with her.

By "quality time," I mean giving someone your undivided attention. I don't mean sitting on the couch watching television together. When you spend time that way, Netflix or HBO has your attention—not your spouse. What I mean is sitting on the couch with the TV off, looking at each other and talking, devices put away, giving each other your undivided attention. It means taking a walk, just the two of you, or going out to eat and looking at each other and talking.

Time is a precious commodity. We all have multiple demands on our time, yet each of us has the exact same hours in a day. We can make the most of those hours by committing some of them to our spouse. If your mate's primary love language is quality time, she simply wants you, being with her, spending time.

Provided it's the right kind of time.

Have you ever noticed that in a restaurant, you can almost always tell the difference between a dating couple and a married couple? Dating couples look at each other and talk. Married couples sit there and gaze around the restaurant. You'd think they went there to eat!

When I sit with my wife and give her twenty minutes of my undivided attention and she does the same for me, we are giving each other twenty minutes of life. We will never have those twenty minutes again; we are giving our lives to each other. It is a powerful emotional communicator of love.

One medicine cannot cure all diseases. In my advice to Andrea and Mark, I made a serious mistake. I assumed that words of affirmation would mean as much to her as they would to him. I had hoped that if each of them would give adequate verbal affirmation, the emotional climate would change, and both of them would begin to feel loved. It worked for Mark. He began to feel more positive about Andrea, sensing her genuine appreciation for his hard work, but it had not worked as well for Andrea, because words of affirmation was not her primary love language. Her language was quality time.

I called Mark, who told me Andrea was still not very happy. "I think I know why," I said. "The problem is that I suggested the wrong love language."

Mark hadn't the foggiest idea what I meant. I explained that what makes one person feel loved emotionally is not always the thing that makes another person feel loved emotionally.

He agreed that his language was words of affirmation. He told me how much that had meant to him as a boy and how good he felt when his wife expressed appreciation for the things he did. I explained that Andrea's language was not words of affirmation but quality time. I explained the concept of giving someone your undivided attention, not talking to her while you watch sports or read texts but looking into her eyes, giving her your full attention, doing something with her that *she* enjoys doing and doing it wholeheartedly. "Like going to the symphony with her," he said. I could tell the lights were coming on in Little Rock.

"Dr. Chapman, that's what she has always complained about. I didn't do things with her; I didn't spend any time with her. She'd always say, 'We used to go places and do things before we were married, but now, you're too busy.' That's her love language all right; no question about it. But what am I gonna do? My job is so demanding."

"Tell me about it," I said.

For the next ten minutes, he gave me the history of his climb up the organizational ladder, of how hard he had worked, and how proud he was of his accomplishments. He told me of his dreams for the future and that he knew that within the next five years, he would be where he wanted to be.

> "She doesn't really hate your job. She hates the fact that she feels so little love coming from you."

"Do you want to be there alone, or do you want to be there with Andrea and the children?" I asked.

"I want her to be with me, Dr. Chapman. I want her to enjoy it with me. That's why it always hurts so much when she criticizes me for spending time on the job. I am doing it for us. I wanted her to be a part of it, but she's always so negative."

"Are you beginning to see why she was so negative, Mark?" I asked. "Her love language is quality time. You have given her so little time that her love tank is empty. She doesn't feel secure in your love. Therefore she has lashed out at what was taking your time in her mind—your job. She doesn't really hate your job. She hates the fact that she feels so little love coming from you. There's only one answer, Mark, and it's costly. You have to make time for Andrea. You have to love her in the right love language."

"I know you are right, Dr. Chapman. Where do I begin?"

I asked Mark if he had his legal pad handy—the same pad on which he had listed positive things about Andrea.

"It's right here."

"Good. We're going to make another list. What are some things that you know Andrea would like you to do with her? Things she has mentioned through the years." Here is Mark's list:

- Spend a weekend in the mountains (sometimes with the kids and sometimes just the two of us).

- Meet her for lunch (at a nice restaurant or sometimes just at Panera).

- When I come home at night, sit down and talk with her about my day and listen as she tells me about her day. (She doesn't want me to watch TV while we are trying to talk.)

- Spend time talking with the children about their school experiences.

- Spend time playing games with the children.

- Go on a picnic with her and the kids on Saturday and don't complain about the ants and the flies.

- Take a vacation with the family at least once a year.
- Go walking with her and talk as we walk.

When Mark's list was finished, I said, "You know what I am going to suggest, don't you, Mark?"

"Do them," he said.

"That's right, one a week for the next two months. Where will you find the time? You will make it. You are a wise man," I continued. "You would not be where you are if you were not a good decision maker. You have the ability to plan your life and to include Andrea in your plans."

"I know," he said. "I can do it."

"And, Mark, this does not have to diminish your vocational goals. It just means that when you get to the top, Andrea and the children will be with you."

"That's what I want more than anything," Mark said with feeling.

The years have come and gone. Andrea and Mark have had ups and downs, but the important thing is that they have done it all together. The children have left the nest, and Mark and Andrea agree that these are their best years ever. Mark has become an avid symphony fan, and Andrea has made an unending list in her legal pad of things she appreciates about Mark. He never tires of hearing them.

FOCUSED ATTENTION

It isn't enough to just be in the same room with someone. A key ingredient in giving your spouse quality time is giving them focused attention, especially in this era of many distractions. When a father is sitting on the floor, rolling a ball to his two-year-old, his attention is not focused on the ball but on his child. For that brief moment, however long it lasts, they are together. If, however, the father is talking on the phone while he rolls the ball, his attention is diluted. Some husbands and wives think they are spending time together when, in reality, they are only living in close proximity. They are in the same house at the same time, but they are not together. A wife who is texting while her husband tries to talk to her is not giving him quality time, because he does not have her full attention.

Quality time does not mean that we have to spend our together moments gazing into each other's eyes. It means that we are doing something together and that we are giving our full attention to the other person. The activity in which we are both engaged is incidental. The important thing emotionally is that we are spending focused time with each other. The activity is a vehicle that creates the sense of togetherness. The important thing about the father rolling the ball to the two-year-old is not the activity itself but the emotions that are created between the father and his child.

Similarly, a husband and wife going running together, if it is genuine quality time, will focus not on the run but on the fact that they are spending time together. What happens on the emotional level is what matters. Our spending time together in a common pursuit communicates that we care about each other, that we enjoy being with each other, that we like to do things together.

QUALITY CONVERSATION

Like words of affirmation, the language of quality time also has many dialects. One of the most common dialects is that of *quality conversation*. By quality conversation, I mean sympathetic dialogue where two individuals are sharing their experiences, thoughts, feelings, and desires in a friendly, uninterrupted context. Most individuals who complain that their spouse does not talk do not mean literally that he or she never says a word. They mean that he or she seldom takes part in sympathetic dialogue. If your spouse's primary love language is quality time, such dialogue is crucial to his or her emotional sense of being loved.

Quality conversation is quite different from the first love language. Words of affirmation focus on what we are saying, whereas quality conversation focuses on what we are hearing. If I am sharing my love for you by means of quality time and we are going to spend that time in conversation, it means I will focus on drawing you out, listening sympathetically to what you have to say. I will ask questions, not in a badgering manner but with a genuine desire to understand your thoughts, feelings, and desires.

I met Patrick when he was forty-three and had been married for seventeen years. I remember him because his first words were so dramatic. He sat in the leather chair in my office and after briefly introducing himself, he leaned forward and said with great emotion, "Dr. Chapman, I have been a fool, a real fool."

"What has led you to that conclusion?" I asked.

"I've been married for seventeen years," he said, "and my wife has left me. Now I realize what a fool I've been."

I repeated my original question, "In what way have you been a fool?"

"My wife would come home from work and tell me about the problems in her office. I would listen to her and then tell her what I thought she should do. I always gave her advice. I told her she had to confront the problem. 'Problems don't go away. You have to talk with the people involved or your supervisor. You have to deal with problems.' The next day she would come home from work and tell me about the same problems. I would ask her if she did what I had suggested the day before. She would shake her head and say no.

"After three or four nights of that, I would get angry. I would tell her not to expect any sympathy from me if she wasn't willing to take the advice I was giving her. She didn't have to live under that kind of stress and pressure. She could solve the problem if she would simply do what I told her. It hurt me to see her living under such stress because I knew she didn't have to. The next time she'd bring up the problem, I would say, 'I don't want to hear about it. I've told you what you need to do. If you're not going to listen to my advice, I don't want to hear it.'

> **Learning to listen may be as difficult as learning a foreign language, but learn we must if we want to communicate love.**

"I would withdraw and go about my business. What a fool I was," he said, "what a fool! Now I realize that she didn't want advice when she told me about her struggles at work. She wanted sympathy. She wanted me to listen, to give her attention, to let her know that I could understand the hurt, the stress, the pressure. She wanted to know that I loved her and that I was with her. She didn't want advice; she just wanted to know that I understood. But I never tried to understand. I was too busy giving advice. And now she's gone."

Patrick's wife had been pleading for quality conversation. Emotionally, she longed for him to focus attention on her by listening to her pain and frustration. Patrick was not focusing on listening but on speaking. He listened only long enough to hear the problem and formulate a solution. He didn't listen long enough or well enough to hear her cry for support and understanding.

Many of us are like Patrick. We are trained to analyze problems and create solutions. We forget that marriage is a relationship, not a project to be completed or a problem to solve. A relationship calls for sympathetic listening with a view to understanding the other person's thoughts, feelings, and desires. We must be willing to give advice but only when it is requested and never in a condescending manner. Most of us have little training in listening. We are far more efficient in thinking and speaking. Learning to listen may be as difficult as learning a foreign language, but learn we must, if we want to communicate love. That is especially true if your spouse's primary love language is quality time and his or her dialect is quality conversation. Fortunately, numerous books and articles have been written on developing the art of listening. I will not seek to repeat what is written elsewhere but suggest the following summary of practical tips.

1. Maintain eye contact when your spouse is talking. That keeps your mind from wandering and communicates that he/she has your full attention.

2. Don't listen to your spouse and do something else at the same time. Remember, quality time is giving someone your undivided attention. If you are doing something you cannot turn from immediately, tell your spouse the truth. A positive approach might be, "I know you are trying to talk to me and I'm interested, but I want to give you my full attention. I can't do that right now, but if you will give me ten minutes to finish this, I'll sit down and listen to you." Most spouses will respect such a request.

3. Listen for feelings. Ask yourself, "What emotion is my spouse experiencing?" When you think you have the answer, confirm

it. For example, "It sounds to me like you are feeling disappointed because I forgot _____." That gives him the chance to clarify his feelings. It also communicates that you are listening intently to what he is saying.

4. Observe body language. Clenched fists, trembling hands, tears, furrowed brows, and eye movements may give you clues as to what the other is feeling. Sometimes body language speaks one message while words speak another. Ask for clarification to make sure you know what she is really thinking and feeling.

5. Refuse to interrupt. Research has indicated that the average individual listens for only seventeen seconds before interrupting and interjecting his own ideas. If I give you my undivided attention while you are talking, I will refrain from defending myself or hurling accusations at you or dogmatically stating my position. My goal is to discover your thoughts and feelings. My objective is not to defend myself or to set you straight. It is to understand you.

LEARNING TO TALK

Quality conversation requires not only sympathetic listening but also self-revelation. When a wife says, "I wish my husband would talk. I never know what he's thinking or feeling," she is pleading for intimacy. She wants to feel close to her husband, but how can she feel close to someone whom she doesn't know? In order for her to feel loved, he must learn to reveal himself. If her primary love language is quality time and her dialect is quality conversation, her emotional love tank will never be filled until he tells her his thoughts and feelings.

Self-revelation does not come easy for some of us. We may have grown up in homes where the expression of thoughts and feelings was not encouraged but squelched. To request a toy was to receive a lecture on the sad state of family finances. The child went away feeling guilty for having the desire, and he quickly learned not to express his desires. When he expressed anger, the parents responded with harsh and condemning words. Thus, the child learned that expressing angry feelings is not appropriate. If the child was made to feel guilty for expressing disappointment at not being able to go to the store with his father, he learned to hold his disappointment inside. By the time we reach adulthood, many of us have learned to deny our feelings. We are no longer in touch with our emotional selves.

A wife says to her husband, "How did you feel about what Steve did?" And the husband responds, "I think he was wrong. He should have—" but he is not telling her his feelings. He is voicing his thoughts. Perhaps he has reason to feel angry or disappointed, but he has lived so long in the world of thought that he does not acknowledge his feelings. When he decides to learn the language of quality conversation, it will be like learning a foreign language. The place to begin is by getting in touch with his feelings, becoming aware that he is an emotional creature in spite of the fact that he has denied that part of his life.

If you need to learn the language of quality conversation, begin by noting the emotions you feel away from home. Carry a small notepad and keep it with you daily. Three times each day, ask yourself, "What emotions have I felt in the last three hours? What did I feel on the way to work when the driver behind me was riding my bumper? What did I feel when I stopped at the gas station and the automatic pump did not shut off and the side of the car was covered in gas? What did I feel when I got to the office and found that the project I was working on had to be completed in three days when I thought I had another two weeks?"

Write down your feelings in the notepad and a word or two to help you remember the event corresponding to the feeling. Your list may look like this:

Event	Feelings
• tailgater	• angry
• gas station	• very upset
• work project due	• frustrated and anxious

Do that exercise three times a day and you will develop an awareness of your emotional nature. Using your notepad, communicate your emotions and the events briefly with your spouse as many days as possible. In a few weeks, you will become comfortable expressing your emotions with him or her. And eventually you will feel comfortable discussing your emotions toward your spouse, the children, and events that occur within the home. Remember, emotions themselves are neither good nor bad. They are simply our psychological responses to the events of life.

Based on our thoughts and emotions, we eventually make decisions. When the tailgater was following you on the highway and you felt angry, perhaps you had these thoughts: I wish he would lay off; I wish he would pass me; if I thought I wouldn't get caught, I'd press the accelerator and leave him in the twilight; I should slam on my brakes and let his insurance company buy me a new car; maybe I'll pull off the road and let him pass.

Eventually, you made some decision or the other driver backed off, turned, or passed you, and you arrived safely at work. In each of life's events, we have emotions, thoughts, desires, and eventually actions. The expression of that process is called self-revelation. If you choose to learn the love dialect of quality conversation, that is the learning road you must follow.

DEAD SEAS AND BABBLING BROOKS

Not all of us are out of touch with our emotions, but when it comes to talking, all of us are affected by our personality. I have observed two basic personality types. The first I call the "Dead Sea." In the little nation of Israel, the Sea of Galilee flows south by way of the Jordan River into the Dead Sea. The Dead Sea goes nowhere. It receives but it does not give. This personality type receives many experiences, emotions, and thoughts throughout the day. They have a large reservoir where they store that information, and they are perfectly happy not to talk. If you say to a Dead Sea personality, "What's wrong? Why aren't you talking tonight?" he will probably answer, "Nothing's wrong. What makes you think something's wrong?" And that response is perfectly honest. He is content not to talk. He could drive from Chicago to Detroit and never say a word and be perfectly happy.

On the other extreme is the "Babbling Brook." For this personality, whatever enters into the eye gate or the ear gate comes out the mouth gate and there are seldom sixty seconds between the two. Whatever they see, whatever they hear, they tell. In fact, if no one is at home to talk to, they will call someone else. "Do you know what I saw? Do you know what I heard?" If they can't get someone on the phone, they may talk to themselves because they have no reservoir. Many times a Dead Sea marries a Babbling Brook. That happens because when they are dating, it is a very attractive match.

If you are a Dead Sea and you date a Babbling Brook, you will have a wonderful evening. You don't have to think, "How will I get the conversation started tonight? How will I keep the conversation flowing?" In fact, you don't have to think at all. All you have to do is nod your head and say, "Uh-huh," and she will fill up the whole evening and you will go home saying, "What a wonderful person." On the other hand, if you are a Babbling Brook and you date a Dead Sea, you will have an equally wonderful evening because Dead Seas are the world's best listeners. You will babble for three hours. He will listen intently to you, and you will go home saying, "What a wonderful person." You attract each other. But five years after marriage, the Babbling Brook wakes up one morning and says, "We've been married five years, and I don't know him." The Dead Sea is saying, "I know her too well. I wish she would stop the flow and give me a break." The good news is that Dead Seas can learn to talk and Babbling Brooks can learn to listen. We are influenced by our personality but not controlled by it.

One way to learn new patterns is to establish a daily sharing time in which each of you will talk about three things that happened to you that day and how you feel about them. I call that the "Minimum Daily Requirement" for a healthy marriage. If you will start with the daily minimum, in a few weeks or months you may find quality conversation flowing more freely between you.

QUALITY ACTIVITIES

In addition to the basic love language of quality time, or giving your spouse your undivided attention, is another dialect called quality activities. At a recent marriage seminar, I asked couples to complete the following sentence: "I feel most loved by my husband/wife when _____." Here is the response of a twenty-nine-year-old husband who has been married for eight years: "I feel most loved by my wife when we do things together, things I like to do and things she likes to do. We talk more. It sorta feels like we are dating again." That is a typical response of individuals whose primary love language is quality time. The emphasis is on being together, doing things together, giving each other undivided attention.

Quality activities may include anything in which one or both of you have an interest. The emphasis is not on what you are doing but on why you are doing it. The purpose is to experience something together, to walk away from it feeling like, "He cares about me. He was willing to do something with me that I enjoy, and he did it with a positive attitude." That is love, and for some people it is love's loudest voice.

One of Emily's favorite pastimes is browsing in used bookstores. "I love to just disappear into the stacks and see what treasures I can find," she says. Husband Jeff, less of an avid reader, has learned to share these experiences with Emily and even point out books she may enjoy. Emily, for her part, has learned to compromise and not force Jeff to spend hours in the stacks. As a result, Jeff proudly says, "I vowed early on that if there was a book Emily wanted, I would buy it for her." Jeff may never become a bookworm, but he has become proficient at loving Emily.

Quality activities may include putting in a garden, visiting historic sites, birding, going to a concert, working out together, or having another couple over for homemade soup and bread. The activities are limited only by your interest and willingness to try new experiences. The essential ingredients in a quality activity are: (1) at least one of you wants to do it, (2) the other is willing to do it, (3) both of you know why you are doing it—to express love by being together.

One of the by-products of quality activities is that they provide a memory bank from which to draw in the years ahead. Fortunate is the couple who remembers a foggy early-morning stroll along the coast, the spring they put in a prairie garden, the day they revisited their childhood neighborhood, the night they attended their first major-league baseball game together, the one and only time they went skiing together and he broke his leg, the quiet times of working side by side at night in their home office, and oh yes, the awe of standing beneath the waterfall after the two-mile hike. They can almost feel the mist as they remember. Those are memories of love, especially for the person whose primary love language is quality time.

And where do we find time for such activities, especially if both of us have vocations outside the home? We make time, just as we make time for lunch and dinner. Why? Because it is just as essential to our marriage as meals are to our health. Is it difficult? Does it take careful planning? Yes. Does it mean we have to give up some individual activities? Perhaps. Does it mean we do some things we don't particularly enjoy? Certainly (see Jeff and Emily). Is it worth it? Without a doubt. What's in it for me? The pleasure of living with a spouse who feels loved and knowing that I have learned to speak his or her love language fluently.

A personal word of thanks to Mark and Andrea in Little Rock, who taught me the value of love language number one, words of affirmation, and love language number two, quality time. Now, it's on to Chicago and love language number three.

YOUR TURN

What in your marriage detracts from spending quality time?

IF YOUR SPOUSE'S LOVE LANGUAGE IS QUALITY TIME:

1. Some couples are together a lot more than others. If that's the case for you, don't try to make all your time together "quality time." Designate specific times and places for planned togetherness.

2. Ask your spouse for a list of five activities that he would enjoy doing with you—don't assume you know. Make plans to do one of them each month for the next five months. If money is an issue, space the freebies between the "we can't afford this" events.

3. One way to share quality time at a distance is to include your spouse in your day as it is happening. Send a photo of something you saw on your walk to the office or relay a funny incident that happened in a meeting. One woman said, "My husband sent a photo of him, my daughter, and the dog sitting on our front porch. I was at work and it made me feel like I was hanging out with them."

4. Think of an activity your spouse enjoys, but which brings little pleasure to you: SEC football, crafting, nature photography. Tell your spouse that you are trying to broaden your horizons and would like to join them in this activity sometime this month. Set a date and give it your best effort.

5. Plan a weekend getaway just for the two of you sometime within the next six months. Be sure it is a weekend when you won't have to be in touch with the office or have a family commitment. Focus on relaxing together doing what one or both of you enjoy.

6. Make time every day to share with each other some of the events of the day. When you spend more time watching the news than you do listening to each other, you end up more concerned about the Middle East than about your spouse. Or: When you spend more time on Facebook than you do listening to each other, you end up more concerned about your hundred "friends" than about your spouse.

7. You have to do chores anyway, so talk as you dust, declutter, and do laundry. It will make the work go much faster!

8. Read the travel section in the Sunday paper together and dream out loud about places you'd like to go. Whether you actually go to these places or not, it's fun to imagine together.

RECEIVING GIFTS

6

Love Language #3
Receiving Gifts

Erik spent a year in Kelsey's "friend zone" before she agreed to go out with him. Since they were both big baseball fans, Erik took her to a minor-league game in Indianapolis. They were sitting in a grassy area beyond the left-field fence when suddenly a hard-hit drive came their way. Erik jumped up and made an impressive barehanded catch—his first home-run grab ever.

Two days later Kelsey found a gift-wrapped package outside her dorm room. She opened it and found a baseball in a small plastic display case (the kind collectors use). Taped to the inside of the case was a ticket stub from the game. Inscribed on the ball was the date of the game and these words:

1st home-run catch
2nd best thing to happen to me that day

They were married two years after that first date. Fifteen years later that baseball, still in its display case, sits on Kelsey's dresser where she can see it every day. It is the first thing she would grab if the house were on fire.

A REMINDER OF LOVE

When I studied anthropology, I was able to "visit" people groups all over the world. I went to Central America and studied the advanced cultures of the Mayans and the Aztecs. I crossed the Pacific and studied the tribal peoples of Melanesia and Polynesia. I studied the Eskimos of the northern tundra and the aboriginal Ainus of Japan. I examined the cultural patterns surrounding love and marriage and found that in every culture I studied, gift giving was a part of the love-marriage process.

Anthropologists are intrigued by cultural patterns that tend to pervade cultures, and so was I. Could it be that gift giving is a fundamental expression of love that transcends cultural barriers?

One of my anthropology field trips was to the island of Dominica. Our purpose was to study the culture of the Carib Indians, and on the trip I met Fred. Fred was not a Carib but a young black man of twenty-eight years. Fred had lost a hand in a fishing-by-dynamite accident. Since the accident, he could not continue his fishing career. He had plenty of available time, and I welcomed his companionship. We spent hours together talking about his culture.

Upon my first visit to Fred's house, he said to me, "Mr. Gary, would you like to have some juice?" to which I responded enthusiastically. He turned to his younger brother and said, "Go get Mr. Gary some juice." His brother turned, walked down the dirt path, climbed a coconut tree, and returned with a green coconut. "Open it," Fred commanded. With three swift movements of the machete, his brother uncorked the coconut, leaving a triangular hole at the top.

Fred handed me the coconut and said, "Juice for you." It was green, but I drank it—all of it—because I knew it was a gift of love. I was his friend, and to friends you give juice.

At the end of our weeks together as I prepared to leave that small island, Fred gave me a final token of his love. It was a crooked stick fourteen inches in length that he had taken from the ocean. It was silky smooth from pounding upon the rocks. Fred said that the stick had lived on the shores of Dominica for a long time, and he wanted me to have it as a reminder of the beautiful island. Even today when I look at that stick, I can almost hear the sound of the Caribbean waves, but it is not as much a reminder of Dominica as it is a reminder of love.

A gift is something you can hold in your hand and say, "Look, he was thinking of me," or, "She remembered me." You must be thinking of someone to give him a gift. The gift itself is a symbol of that thought. It doesn't matter whether it costs money. What is important is that you thought of him. And it is not the thought implanted only in the mind that counts but the thought expressed in actually securing the gift and giving it as the expression of love.

Visual symbols of love are more important to some people than others.

Mothers remember the days their children bring a flower from the yard as a gift. They feel loved, even if it was a dandelion or a flower they didn't want picked. From early years, children are inclined to give gifts to their parents, which may be another indication that gift giving is fundamental to love.

Gifts are visual symbols of love. Most wedding ceremonies include the giving and receiving of rings. The person performing the ceremony says, "These rings are outward and visible signs of an inward and spiritual bond that unites your two hearts in love that has no end." That is not meaningless rhetoric. It is verbalizing a significant truth—symbols have emotional value. Perhaps that is even more graphically displayed near the end of a disintegrating marriage when the husband or wife stops wearing the wedding ring. One husband said, "When she threw her wedding rings at me and angrily walked out of the house, slamming the door behind her, I knew our marriage was in serious trouble. I didn't pick up her rings for two days. When I finally did, I couldn't stop crying." The lonely rings stirred deep emotions within the husband.

Visual symbols of love are more important to some people than to others. That's why individuals have different attitudes toward wedding rings. Some never take the ring off after the wedding. Others don't even wear a wedding band. If receiving gifts is my primary love language, I will place great value on the ring you have given me and I will wear it with pride. I will also be moved emotionally by other gifts that you give through the years. I will see them as expressions of love. Without gifts as visual symbols, I may question your love.

Gifts come in all sizes, colors, and shapes. Some are expensive, and others are free. To the individual whose primary love language is receiving gifts, the cost of the gift will matter little, unless it is out of line with what you can afford. If a millionaire gives only one-dollar gifts regularly, the spouse may question whether that is an expression of love, but when family finances are limited, a one-dollar gift may speak a million dollars worth of love.

Gifts may be purchased, found, or made. The husband who finds an interesting bird feather while out

> **To invest in loving your spouse is to invest in blue-chip stocks.**

jogging and brings it home to his wife has found himself an expression of love, unless, of course, his wife is allergic to feathers. For the man who can afford it, you can purchase a beautiful card for less than five dollars. For the man who cannot, you can make one for free. Get the paper out of the trash can where you work, fold it in the middle, take scissors and cut out a heart, write "I love you," and sign your name. Gifts need not be expensive.

But what of the person who says, "I'm not a gift giver. I didn't receive many gifts growing up. I never learned how to select gifts. It doesn't come naturally for me." Congratulations, you have just made the first discovery in becoming a great lover. You and your spouse speak different love languages. Now that you have made that discovery, get on with the business of learning your second language. If your spouse's primary love language is receiving gifts, you can become a proficient gift giver. In fact, it is one of the easiest love languages to learn.

Where do you begin? Make a list of all the gifts your spouse has expressed excitement about receiving through the years. They may be gifts you have given or gifts given by other family members or friends. The list will give you an idea of the kind of gifts your spouse would enjoy receiving. If you have little or no knowledge about selecting the kinds of gifts on your list, recruit the help of family members who know your spouse. In the meantime, select gifts that you feel comfortable purchasing, making, or finding, and give them to your spouse. Don't wait for a special occasion. If receiving gifts is his/her primary love language, almost anything you give will be received as an expression of love. (If she has been critical of your gifts in the past and almost nothing you have given has been acceptable, then receiving gifts is almost certainly not her primary love language.)

THE BEST INVESTMENT

If you are to become an effective gift giver, you may have to change your attitude about money. Each of us has an individualized perception of the purposes of money, and we have various emotions associated with spending it. Some of us have a spending orientation. We feel good about ourselves when we are spending money. Others have a saving and investing perspective. We feel good about ourselves when we are saving money and investing it wisely.

If you are a spender, you will have little difficulty purchasing gifts for your spouse; but if you are a saver, you will experience emotional resistance to the idea of spending money as an expression of love. You don't purchase things for yourself. Why should you purchase things for your spouse? But that attitude fails to recognize that you are purchasing things for yourself. By saving and investing money, you are purchasing self-worth and emotional security. You are caring for your own emotional needs in the way you handle money. What you are not doing is meeting the emotional needs of your spouse. If you discover that your spouse's primary love language is receiving gifts, then perhaps you will understand that purchasing gifts for him or her is the best investment you can make. You are investing in your relationship and filling your spouse's emotional love tank, and with a full love tank, he or she will likely reciprocate emotional love to you in a language you will understand. When both persons' emotional needs are met, your marriage will take on a whole new dimension. Don't worry about your savings. You will always be a saver, but to invest in loving your spouse is to invest in blue-chip stocks.

THE GIFT OF SELF

There is an intangible gift that sometimes speaks more loudly than a gift that can be held in one's hand. I call it the gift of self or the gift of presence. Being there when your spouse needs you speaks loudly to the one whose primary love language is receiving gifts. Sonia once said to me, "My husband loves softball more than he loves me."

"Why do you say that?" I inquired.

"On the day our baby was born, he played softball. I was lying in the hospital all afternoon while he played softball," she said.

"Was he there when the baby was born?"

"He stayed long enough for the baby to be born, but ten minutes afterward, he left. It was awful. It was such an important moment in our lives. I wanted us to share it together. I wanted Tony to be there with me."

That "baby" was now fifteen years old, and Sonia was talking about the event with all the emotion as though it had happened yesterday. I probed further. "Have you based your conclusion that Tony loves softball more than he loves you on this one experience?"

"No," she said. "On the day of my mother's funeral, he also played softball."

"Did he go to the funeral?"

"Yes, he did. He went to the funeral, but as soon as it was over, he left to get to his game. I couldn't believe it. My brothers and sisters came to the house with me, but my husband was playing softball."

Later, I asked Tony about those two events. He knew exactly what I was talking about. "I knew she would bring that up," he said. "I was there through all the labor and when the baby was born. I took pictures; I was so happy. I couldn't wait to tell the guys on the team, but my bubble was burst when I got back to the hospital that evening.

> If the physical presence of your spouse is important to you, I urge you to verbalize that to your spouse.

She was furious with me. I couldn't believe what she was saying. I thought she would be proud of me for telling the team.

"And when her mother died? She probably didn't tell you that I took off work a week before she died and spent the whole week at the hospital and at her mother's house doing repairs and helping out. After she died and the funeral was over, I felt I had done all I could do. I needed a breather. I like to play softball, and I knew that would help me relax and relieve some of the stress I'd been under. I thought she would want me to take a break.

"I had done what I thought was important to her, but it wasn't enough. She has never let me forget those two days. She says that I love softball more than I love her. That's ridiculous."

He was a sincere husband who failed to understand the tremendous power of presence. His being there for his wife was more important than anything else in her mind. Physical presence in the time of crisis is the most powerful gift you can give if your spouse's primary love language is receiving gifts. Your body becomes the symbol of your love. Remove the symbol, and the sense of love evaporates. In counseling, Tony and Sonia worked through the hurts and misunderstandings of the past. Eventually, Sonia was able to forgive him, and Tony came to understand why his presence was so important to her.

If the physical presence of your spouse is important to you, I urge you to verbalize that to your spouse. Don't expect him to read your mind. If, on the other hand, your spouse says to you, "I really want you to be there with me tonight, tomorrow, this afternoon," take his request seriously. From your perspective, it may not be important; but if you are not responsive to that request, you may be communicating a message you do not intend. A husband once said, "When my mother died, my wife's supervisor said that she could be off two hours for the funeral, but she needed to be back in the office for the afternoon. My wife told him that she felt her husband needed her support that day and she would have to be away the entire day. The supervisor replied, 'If you are gone all day, you may well lose your job.'

"My wife said, 'My husband is more important than my job.' She spent the day with me. Somehow that day, I felt more loved by her than ever before. I have never forgotten what she did.

"Incidentally, she didn't lose her job. Her supervisor soon left, and she was asked to take his job." That wife had spoken the love language of her husband, and he never forgot it.

MIRACLE IN CHICAGO

Almost everything ever written on the subject of love indicates that at the heart of love is the spirit of giving. All five love languages challenge us to give to our spouse, but for some, receiving gifts, visible symbols of love, speaks the loudest. I heard the most graphic illustration of that truth in Chicago, where I met Doug and Kate.

They attended my marriage seminar and agreed to take me to O'Hare Airport after the seminar on Saturday afternoon. We had two or three hours before my flight, and they asked if I would like to stop at a restaurant. I was famished, so I readily assented.

Kate began talking almost immediately after we sat down. She said, "Dr. Chapman, God used you to perform a miracle in our marriage. Three years ago, we attended your marriage seminar here in Chicago for the first time. I was desperate," she said. "I was thinking seriously of leaving Doug and had told him so. Our marriage had been empty for a long time. I had given up. For years, I had complained to Doug that I needed his love, but he never responded. I loved the children, and I knew they loved me, but I felt nothing coming from Doug. In fact, by that time, I hated him. He was a methodical person. He did everything by routine. He was as predictable as a clock, and no one could break into his routine.

"For years," she continued, "I tried to be a good wife. I did all the things I thought a good wife should do. I had sex with him because I knew that was important to him, but I felt no love coming from him. I felt like he stopped dating me after we got married and simply took me for granted. I felt used and unappreciated.

"When I talked to Doug about my feelings, he'd laugh at me and say we had as good a marriage as anybody else in the community. He didn't understand why I was so unhappy. He would remind me that the bills were paid, that we had a nice house and a new car, that I was free to work or not work outside the home, and that I should be happy instead of complaining all the time. He didn't even try to understand my feelings. I felt totally rejected.

"Well, anyway," she said as she moved her tea and leaned forward, "we came to your seminar three years ago. I did not know what to expect, and frankly I didn't expect much. I didn't think anybody could change Doug. During and after the seminar, he didn't say too much. He seemed to like it. Then that Monday afternoon, he came home from work and gave me a rose. 'Where did you get that?' I asked. 'I bought it from a street vendor,' he said. 'I thought you deserved a rose.' I started crying. 'Oh, Doug, that is so sweet of you.'

"On Tuesday he texted me from the office at about one thirty and asked me what I thought about his picking up a pizza for dinner. That may not sound like a big deal to most people, but Doug never does anything like that. I told him I thought the idea was wonderful, and so he brought home a pizza and we all had a fun time together. I gave him a hug and told him how much I enjoyed it.

"When he came home on Wednesday, he brought each of the kids a box of Cracker Jacks, and he had a small potted plant for me. He said he knew the rose would die, and he thought I might like something that would be around for a while. I was beginning to think I was hallucinating! I couldn't believe what Doug was doing or why he was doing it.

"Thursday night after dinner, he handed me a card with a message about his not always being able to express his love to me but hoping that the card would communicate how much he cared. 'Why don't we get a babysitter on Saturday night and the two of us go out for dinner?' he suggested. 'That would be great,' I said. On Friday afternoon, he stopped by the cookie shop and bought each of us one of our favorite cookies. Again, he kept it as a surprise, telling us only that he had a treat for dessert.

"By Saturday night," she said, "I was in orbit. I had no idea what had come over Doug, or if it would last, but I was enjoying every minute of it. After our dinner at the restaurant, I said to him, 'Doug, you have to tell me what's happening. I don't understand.'"

She looked at me intently. "Dr. Chapman, this was a man who never gave me a gift, ever. He never gave me a card for any occasion. He always said, 'It's a waste of money; you look at the card and throw it away.' He never bought the children anything and expected me to buy only the essentials. He expected me to have dinner ready every night. I mean, this was a radical change in his behavior."

I turned to Doug and asked, "What did you say to her in the restaurant when she asked you what was going on?"

"I told her that I had listened to your lecture on love languages at the seminar and that I realized that her love language was gifts. I also realized that I had not given her a gift in years, maybe not since we had been married. I remembered that when we were dating, I used to bring her flowers and other small gifts, but after marriage I figured we couldn't afford that. I told her that I had decided that I was going to try to get her a gift every day for one week and see if it made any difference in her. I had to admit that I had seen a pretty big difference in her attitude during the week.

"I told her that I realized that what you said was really true and that learning the right love language was the key to helping another person feel loved. I said I was sorry that I had been so dense for all those years and had failed to meet her need for love. I told her that I really loved her and that I appreciated all the things she did for me and the kids. I told her that with God's help, I was going to be a gift giver for the rest of my life.

"She said, 'But, Doug, you can't go on buying me gifts every day for the rest of your life. We can't afford that.' 'Well, maybe not every day,' I said, 'but at least once a week. That would be fifty-two more gifts per year than what you have received in the past five years.'"

"I don't think he has missed a single week in three years," Kate said. "He is like a new man. You wouldn't believe how happy we have been. Our children call us lovebirds now. My tank is full and overflowing."

I looked at Doug. "But what about you, Doug? Do you feel loved by Kate?"

"Oh, I've always felt loved by her, Dr. Chapman. She does so much to help me and the kids. She takes care of the finances, knows where we all have to be when, stays in touch with my family on Facebook... I know she loves me." He smiled and said, "Now, you know what my love language is, don't you?"

I did, and I also knew why Kate had used the word *miracle*.

Gifts need not be expensive, nor must they be given weekly. But for some individuals, their worth has nothing to do with monetary value and everything to do with love.

YOUR TURN

Reflect on ways to give gifts even if finances are tight.

IF YOUR SPOUSE'S LOVE LANGUAGE IS
RECEIVING GIFTS:

1. You've heard of the twelve days of Christmas. How about twelve days of gifts for your spouse's birthday or your wedding anniversary?

2. Let nature be your guide: The next time you take a walk through the neighborhood, keep your eyes open for a gift for your spouse. It may be a stone, a stick, or a feather. You may even attach special meaning to your natural gift. For example, a smooth stone may symbolize your marriage with many of the rough places now polished. A feather may symbolize how your spouse is the "wind beneath your wings."

3. Discover the value of "handmade originals." Make a gift for your spouse. This may require you to enroll in an art or crafts class: ceramics, scrapbooking, painting, wood carving. Your main purpose for enrolling is to make your spouse a gift. A handmade gift often becomes a family heirloom.

4. When money is tight, think of appropriate symbolic gifts. Look at pictures of beautiful houses and daydream about what kind of house you would have if money were no object. Instead of plane tickets, go on a "flight of fancy" to Dubai or Sydney.

5. Keep a "Gift Idea Notebook." Every time you hear your spouse say: "I really like that," or "Oh, I would really like to have one of those!" write it down in your notebook. (How many of us have the experience of asking someone what they want for their birthday or Christmas and getting the response, "Oh, I don't know . . .") Listen carefully and you will get quite a list. This will serve as a guide when you get

ready to select a gift. To prime the pump, you may look through a favorite online shopping site together.

6. Enlist a "personal shopper." If you really don't have a clue as to how to select a gift for your spouse, ask a friend or family member who knows your wife or husband well to help you. Most people enjoy making a friend happy by getting them a gift, especially if it is with your money.

7. Offer the gift of presence during an especially hard time in your spouse's life—perhaps if he's caring for an elderly parent or she's dealing with a job crisis.

8. Give your spouse a book and agree to read it yourself. Then offer to discuss together a chapter each week. Don't choose a book that you want him or her to read. Choose a book on a topic in which you know your spouse has an interest: sex, football, gourmet cuisine, investing, childrearing, religion, history.

9. Give a lasting tribute. Give a gift to your spouse's favorite charity in honor of her birthday, your anniversary, or another occasion. Ask the charity to send a card informing your spouse of what you have done. The church or charity will be excited and so will your spouse.

ACTS OF SERVICE

7

Love Language #4

Acts of Service

Michelle sat in the living room, pecking away at the laptop. She could hear sounds from the utility room, where husband Brad was catching up with the piles of laundry. She smiled to herself. In recent days Brad had cleaned the condo, fixed supper, and run the errands, all because Michelle was in the midst of working on her thesis for grad school. It made her feel content . . . loved.

Michelle's primary love language was what I call "acts of service." By acts of service, I mean doing things you know your spouse would like you to do. You seek to please her by serving her, to express your love for her by doing things for her. So it was with Doug and Kate, whom we met in the last chapter.

Such actions as cooking a meal, setting a table, emptying the dishwasher, vacuuming, changing the baby's diaper, picking up a prescription, keeping the car in operating condition, paying the bills, trimming the shrubs, walking the dog, and dealing with landlords and insurance companies are all acts of service. They require thought, planning, time, effort, and energy. If done with a positive spirit, they are indeed expressions of love.

And they don't necessarily require a lot of time. One man always dreaded the chore of bringing in the garbage cans from the curb at the end of a long workweek. All he wanted to do was go directly in the house, kick off his shoes, and relax. But some nights were different: "As I turned down our street and scanned the horizon for the toppled cans, they were nowhere to be seen. My wife had already taken them into the garage. The empty curb was a clear message to me: 'I was thinking of you. You were with me, even when you were gone.'"[2]

CONVERSATION IN A MILL TOWN

I discovered the impact of acts of service in the little village of China Grove, North Carolina. China Grove sits in central North Carolina, originally nestled in chinaberry trees, not far from Andy Griffith's legendary Mayberry. At the time of this story, China Grove was a textile town with a population of 1,500. I had been away for more than ten years, studying anthropology, psychology, and theology. I was making my semiannual visit to keep in touch with my roots.

Almost everyone I knew except Dr. Shin and Dr. Smith worked in the mill. Dr. Shin was the medical doctor, and Dr. Smith was the dentist. And of course, there was Preacher Blackburn, who was pastor of the church. For most couples in China Grove, life centered on work and church. The conversation at the mill focused on the superintendent's latest decision and how it affected their job in particular. The services at church focused mainly on the anticipated joys of heaven. In that pristine American setting, I discovered love language number four.

Love Language #4: Acts of Service • 93

I was standing under a chinaberry tree after church on Sunday when a young couple approached me. I didn't recognize either of them. I assumed they had grown up while I was away. Introducing himself, Dave said, "I hear you've been studying counseling."

I smiled and said, "Well, a little bit."

"I have a question," he said. "Can a couple make it in marriage if they disagree on everything?"

It was one of those theoretical questions that I knew had a personal root. I went right to the point. "How long have you been married?"

"Two years," he responded. "And we don't agree on anything."

"Give me some examples," I said.

"Well, for one thing, Mary doesn't like me to go hunting. I work all week in the mill, and I like to go hunting on Saturdays—not every Saturday but when hunting season is in."

Mary had been silent until this point when she interjected. "When hunting season is out, he goes fishing, and besides that, he doesn't hunt just on Saturdays. He takes off from work to go hunting."

"Once or twice a year I take off two or three days from work to go hunting in the mountains with some buddies," Dave said, irritated. "What's wrong with that?"

"What else do you disagree on?" I asked.

"Well, she wants me to go to church all the time. I don't mind going on Sunday morning, but Sunday night I like to rest. It's all right if she wants to go, but I don't think I ought to have to go."

Again Mary spoke up. "You don't really want me to go either," she said. "You fuss every time I walk out the door."

I knew that things weren't supposed to be getting this hot under a shady tree in front of a church. As a young, aspiring counselor, I feared that I was getting in over my head, but having been trained to ask questions and listen, I continued. "What other things do you disagree on?"

This time Mary answered. "He wants me to stay home all day and work in the house," she said. "He gets mad if I go see my mother or go shopping or something."

"I don't mind her going to see her mother," he said, "but when I come home, I like to see the house cleaned up. Some weeks, she doesn't make the bed up for three or four days, and half the time, she hasn't even started supper. I work hard, and I like to eat when I get home. Besides that, the house is a wreck," he continued. "The baby's things are all over the floor, the baby is dirty, and I don't like filth. She seems to be happy to live in a pigpen. We don't have very much, and we live in a small mill house, but at least it could be clean."

"What's wrong with him helping me around the house?" Mary asked. "He acts like a husband shouldn't do anything around the house. All he wants to do is work and hunt. He expects me to do everything."

Thinking that I had better start looking for solutions rather than prying for more disagreements, I looked at Dave and asked, "Dave, when you were dating, before you got married, did you go hunting or fishing every Saturday?"

"Pretty much, but I always got home in time to go see her on Saturday night. Most of the time, I'd get home in time to wash my truck before I went to see her. I didn't like to go see her with a dirty truck."

As we continued talking, I learned that Mary had gotten married right out of high school and that during her senior year Dave came to see her almost every night and stayed for supper. "He would help me do my chores around the house and then we'd sit and talk until suppertime."

"Dave, what did the two of you do after supper?" I asked.

He looked up with a sheepish smile and said, "Well, the regular dating stuff, you know."

"But if I had a school project," Mary said, "he'd help me with it. Sometimes we worked hours on school projects. I was in charge of the Christmas float for the senior class. He helped me for three weeks every afternoon. He was great."

I switched gears and focused on the third area of their disagreement. "Dave, when you were dating, did you go to church with Mary on Sunday nights?"

"Yes, I did," he said. "If I didn't go to church with her, I couldn't see her that night. Her father was strict that way."

I thought I was beginning to see some light, but I wasn't sure they were seeing it. I asked Mary, "When you were dating Dave, what convinced you that he really loved you? What made him different from other guys you had dated?"

"It was the way he helped me with everything," she said. "None of the other guys cared about all that. He even helped me wash dishes when he had supper at our house. He was the most incredible person I had ever met, but after we got married that changed."

Turning to Dave, I asked, "Why do you think you did all these things for her before you were married?"

"It just seemed natural for me," he said. "It's what I would want someone to do for me if she cared about me."

"And why do you think you stopped helping her after you got married?" I asked.

"Well, I guess I expected it to be like my family. Dad worked, and Mom took care of things at the house. I never saw my dad do anything around the house. Since Mom stayed home, she did everything—cooking, cleaning, washing, and ironing. I just thought that was the way it was supposed to be."

Now we were getting somewhere. "Dave, a moment ago what did you hear Mary say when I asked her what really made her feel loved by you when you were dating?"

He responded, "Helping her with things and doing things with her."

"So, can you understand how she could feel unloved when you stopped helping her with things?" He was nodding yes. I continued. "It was a normal thing for you to follow the model of your mother and father in marriage. Almost all of us tend to do that, but your behavior toward Mary was a radical change from your courtship. The one thing that had assured her of your love disappeared."

Then I asked Mary, "What did you hear Dave say when I asked, 'Why did you do all of those things to help Mary when you were dating?'"

"He said that it came naturally to him," she replied.

"That's right," I said, "and he also said that is what he would want someone to do for him if she loved him. He was doing those things for you and with you because in his mind that's the way anyone shows love. Once you were married and living in your own house, he had expectations of what you would do if you loved him. You would keep the house clean, you would cook, and so on. In brief, you would do things for him to express your love. When he did not see you doing those things, do you understand why he would feel unloved?" Mary was nodding now too. I continued, "My guess is that the reason you are both so unhappy in your marriage is that neither of

> **No one likes to be forced to do anything. Love is always freely given.**

you is showing your love by doing things for each other."

Mary said, "I think you're right, and the reason I stopped doing things for him is because I didn't like how he bossed me around. It was as if he was trying to make me be like his mother."

"That's it," I said. "No one likes to be forced to do anything. In fact, love is always freely given. Love cannot be demanded. We can request things of each other, but we must never demand anything. Requests give direction to love, but demands stop the flow of love."

Dave looked thoughtful. "I did boss her around—demand, like you said. I guess I was disappointed in her as a wife. I know I said some cruel things, and I understand how she could be upset with me."

"I think things can be turned around rather easily at this juncture," I said. I pulled two note cards out of my pocket. "Let's try something. I want each of you to sit on the steps of the church and make a request list. Dave, I want you to list three or four things that if Mary chose to do them would make you feel loved when you walk into the house in the afternoon. If making the bed is important to you, then put it down. Mary, I want you to make a list of three or four things that you would really like to have Dave's help in doing, things which, if he chose to do them, would help you know that he loved you." (I'm big on lists; they force us to think concretely.)

After five to six minutes, they handed me their lists. Dave's list read:

- Make up the beds every day.
- Have the baby's face washed when I get home.
- Put her shoes in the closet before I get home.
- Try to have supper at least started before I get home so that we could eat within 30 to 45 minutes after I get home.

I read the list out loud and said to Dave, "I'm understanding you to say that if Mary chooses to do these four things, you will view them as acts of love toward you."

"Yeah," he said, "just those four things. That would really make a difference in how I feel about her."

Then I read Mary's list:

- I wish he would wash the car every week instead of expecting me to do it.
- I wish he would change the baby's diaper after he gets home in the afternoon, especially if I am working on supper.
- I wish he would vacuum the house for me once a week.
- I wish he would mow the lawn every week in the summer and not let it get so tall that I'm ashamed of our yard.

I said, "Mary, I am understanding you to say that if Dave chooses to do those four things, you would take his actions as genuine expressions of love toward you."

"I would," she said.

"Can you do what she asks, Dave?"

"Yes," he said.

"Mary, what about you? Can you do the things on Dave's list?"

"Yes, I can. In the past, it always seemed like no matter what I did, it was never enough."

I turned to Dave. "Dave, you understand that what I am suggesting is a change from the model of marriage that your mother and father had."

"Oh, my dad cut the grass and washed the car."

"But he didn't change the diapers or vacuum, right?"

"Never!" he said, grinning.

"You don't have to do these, you understand? If you do them, however, it will be an act of love to Mary."

And to Mary I said, "You understand that you don't have to do these things, but if you want to express love for Dave, here are four ways that will be meaningful to him. I want to suggest that you try these for two months and see if they help. At the end of two months, you may want to add additional requests to your lists and share them with each other. I would not add more than one request per month, however."

"This really makes sense," Mary said. "Thank you," Dave said. They took each other by the hand and walked toward their car. I said to myself out loud, "I think this is what church is all about. I think I am going to enjoy being a counselor." I have never forgotten the insight I gained under that chinaberry tree.

WHAT I LEARNED FROM DAVE AND MARY

After years of research, I have realized what a unique situation Dave and Mary presented me. Seldom do I meet a couple who both have the same love language—in this case, acts of service. But you may be wondering, Then why were they having so much difficulty? The answer lies in the fact that they were speaking different dialects. They were doing things for each other—but not the most *important* things. When Mary and Dave were forced to think concretely, they easily identified their specific dialects, and when they started speaking them, their love tanks began to fill.

It's easy to work at the wrong things. A husband could spend an entire long weekend doing chores—raking leaves, preparing the lawn for winter, winding up hoses and putting them away, winterizing the cars, pulling holiday decorations out of the attic, cutting logs for the fireplace—and not add a drop to his wife's love tank. On the other hand, that same husband could bring home Chinese takeout, clean the kitchen afterward, and then put the kids to bed on his own while his wife was wiped out after a long day—and fill her love tank to overflowing.

Before we leave our mill town friends, I would like to make three other observations. First, they illustrate clearly that what we do for each other before marriage is no indication of what we will do after marriage. Before marriage, we are carried along by the force of the in-love obsession. After marriage, we revert to being the people we were before we "fell in love." Our actions are influenced by the model of our parents; our own personality; our perceptions of love; our emotions, needs, and desires. Only one thing is certain about our behavior: It will not be the same behavior we exhibited when we were caught up in being "in love."

That leads me to the second truth: Love is a choice and cannot be coerced. Dave and Mary were criticizing each other's behavior and getting nowhere. Once they decided to make requests of each other rather than demands, their marriage began to turn around.

Criticism and demands tend to drive wedges. With enough criticism, you may get acquiescence from your spouse. He may do what you want, but probably it will not be an expression of love. You can give guidance to love by making requests: "I wish you would wash the car, change the baby's diaper, mow the grass," but you cannot create the will to love. Each of us must decide daily to love or not to love our spouses. If we choose to love, then expressing it in the way in which our spouse requests will make our love most effective emotionally.

There is a third truth, which only the mature lover will be able to hear. My spouse's criticisms about my behavior provide me with the clearest clue to her primary love language. People tend to criticize their spouse most loudly in the area where they themselves have the deepest emotional need. Their criticism is an ineffective way of pleading for love. If we understand that, it may help us process their criticism in a more productive manner. A wife may say to her husband after he gives her a criticism, "It sounds like that is extremely important to you. Could you explain why it is so crucial?" Criticism often needs clarification. Initiating such a conversation may eventually turn the criticism into a request rather than a demand. Mary's constant condemnation of Dave's hunting was not an expression of her hatred for the sport of hunting. She blamed hunting as the thing that kept him from washing the car, vacuuming the house, and mowing the grass. When he learned to meet her need for love by speaking her emotional love language, she became free to support him in his hunting.

DOORMAT OR LOVER?

"I have served him for twenty years. I have waited on him hand and foot. I have been his doormat while he ignored me, mistreated me, and humiliated me in front of my friends and family. I don't hate him. I wish him no ill, but I resent him, and I no longer wish to live with him." That wife has performed acts of service for twenty years, but they have not been expressions of love. They were done out of fear, guilt, and resentment.

A doormat is an inanimate object. You can wipe your feet on it, step on it, kick it around, or whatever you like. It has no will of its own. It can be your servant but not your lover. When we treat our spouses as objects, we preclude the possibility of love. Manipulation by guilt ("If you were a good spouse, you would do this for me") is not the language of love. Coercion by fear ("You will do this or you will be sorry") is alien to love. No person should ever be a doormat. We may allow ourselves to be used, but we are in fact creatures of emotion, thoughts, and desires. And we have the ability to make decisions and take action. Allowing oneself to be used or manipulated by another is not an act of love. It is, in fact, an act of treason. You are allowing him or her to develop inhumane habits. Love says, "I love you too much to let you treat me this way. It is not good for you or me."

Learning the love language of acts of service will require some of us to reexamine our stereotypes of the roles of husbands and wives. These have changed over the last several decades, but models from our past can linger, and different cultures have different expectations of the "right" way things are done in marriage.

To Dave's credit, he was willing to break from his expectations when he realized how important it was to Mary. That is necessary for all of us if our spouse's primary love language asks something of us that seems inappropriate to our role.

A willingness to examine and change stereotypes is necessary in order to express love more effectively. Remember, there are no rewards for maintaining stereotypes, but there are tremendous benefits to meeting the emotional needs of your spouse. If your spouse's love language is acts of service, then "actions speak louder than words."

Now let's move on to love language number five.

YOUR TURN

Many acts of service will involve household chores, but not all. What are some non-chore ways of serving your mate?

IF YOUR SPOUSE'S LOVE LANGUAGE IS
ACTS OF SERVICE:

1. Consider serving someone (or something) your spouse loves: an older relative, caring attentively for a pet, a favorite cause.

2. Print note cards with the following:

   "Today I will show my love for you by . . ." Complete the sentence with a task you know your spouse would love you to do: picking up the clutter, taking old clothes to a thrift store, fixing something that's been broken a long time, weeding the garden. (Bonus points if it's a chore that's been put off.)

3. Ask your spouse to make a list of ten things he or she would like for you to do during the next month. Then ask your spouse to prioritize those by numbering them 1–10, with 1 being the most important and 10 being least important. Use this list to plan your strategy for a month of love. (Get ready to live with a happy spouse.)

4. While your spouse is away, get the children to help you with some act of service for him. When he walks in the door, join the children in shouting, "Surprise! We love you!" Then share your act of service.

5. This can also work when your spouse is away for a long period of time, such as a military deployment. Recruit the kids to help you with some act of service for him. Take a picture of the results and send it—or, even better, show it to him via Skype and yell, "Surprise! We love you!"

6. If your requests to your mate come across as nags or putdowns, try writing them in words that would be less offensive to them. Share this revised wording with your

spouse. For example, "The yard always looks so nice, and I really appreciate your work. I'd love to thank you in advance for mowing the lawn this week before Paul and Amy come over for dinner." Your husband might even respond, "Where's the lawnmower, I can't wait!" Try it and see.

7. If you have more money than time, hire someone to do the acts of service that neither of you wants to do, such as the yard work or a once-a-month deep cleaning of your home.

8. Run interference for your spouse during his or her favorite TV show or important sports event. Take care of all the phone calls, kid emergencies, and so on.

PHYSICAL TOUCH

8

LOVE LANGUAGE #5
Physical Touch

We have long known that physical touch is a way of communicating emotional love. Numerous research projects in the area of child development have made that conclusion: Babies who are held, stroked, and kissed develop a healthier emotional life than those who are left for long periods of time without physical contact.

Physical touch is also a powerful vehicle for communicating marital love. Holding hands, kissing, embracing, and sexual intercourse are all ways of communicating emotional love to one's spouse. For some individuals, physical touch is their primary love language. Without it, they feel unloved. With it, their emotional tank is filled, and they feel secure in the love of their spouse.

THE POWER OF TOUCH

Of the five senses, touching, unlike the other four, is not limited to one localized area of the body. Tiny tactile receptors are located throughout the body. When those receptors are touched or pressed, nerves carry impulses to the brain. The brain interprets these impulses and we perceive that the thing that touched us is warm or cold, hard or soft. It causes pain or pleasure. We may also interpret it as loving or hostile.

Some parts of the body are more sensitive than others. The difference is due to the fact that the tiny tactile receptors are not scattered evenly over the body but arranged in clusters. Thus, the tip of the tongue is highly sensitive to touch whereas the back of the shoulders is the least sensitive. The tips of the fingers and the tip of the nose are other extremely sensitive areas. Our purpose, however, is not to understand the neurological basis of the sense of touch but rather its psychological importance.

Physical touch can make or break a relationship. It can communicate hate or love. To the person whose primary love language is physical touch, the message will be far louder than the words "I hate you" or "I love you." A slap in the face is detrimental to any child, but it is devastating to a child whose primary love language is touch. A tender hug communicates love to any child, but it shouts love to the child whose primary love language is physical touch. The same is true of adults.

In marriage, the touch of love may take many forms. Since touch receptors are located throughout the body, lovingly touching your spouse almost anywhere can be an expression of love. That does not mean that all touches are created equal. Some will bring more pleasure to your spouse than others. Your best instructor is your spouse, of course. After all, she is the one you are seeking to love. She knows best what she perceives as a loving touch. Don't insist on touching her in your way and in your time. Learn to speak her love dialect.

Your spouse may find some touches uncomfortable or irritating. To insist on continuing those touches is to communicate the opposite of love. It is saying that you are not sensitive to her needs and that you care little about her perceptions of what is pleasant. Don't make the mistake of believing that the touch that brings pleasure to you will also bring pleasure to her.

Love touches may be explicit and demand your full attention, such as in a back rub or sexual foreplay, culminating in intercourse. On the other hand, love touches may be implicit and require only a moment, such as putting your hand on his shoulder as you pour a cup of coffee or rubbing your body against him as you pass in the kitchen. Explicit love touches obviously take more time, not only in actual touching but in developing your understanding of how to communicate love to your spouse this way. If a back massage communicates love loudly to your spouse, then the time, money, and energy you spend in learning to be a good masseur or masseuse will be well invested. If sexual intercourse is your mate's primary dialect, reading about and discussing the art of sexual lovemaking will enhance your expression of love.

> **Coming up with new ways and places to touch can be an exciting challenge.**

Implicit love touches require little time but much thought, especially if physical touch is not your primary love language and if you did not grow up in a "touching family." Sitting close to each other as you watch your favorite television program requires no additional time but may communicate your love loudly. Touching your spouse as you walk through the room where he is sitting takes only a moment. Touching each other when you leave the house and again when you return may involve only a brief kiss or hug but will speak volumes to your spouse.

Once you discover that physical touch is the primary love language of your spouse, you are limited only by your imagination on ways to express love. Coming up with new ways and places to touch can be an exciting challenge. If you have not been an "under-the-table toucher," you might find that it will add a spark to your dining out. If you are not accustomed to holding hands in public, you may find that you can fill your spouse's emotional love tank as you stroll through the parking lot. If you don't normally kiss as soon as you get into the car together, you may find that it will greatly enhance your travels. Hugging your spouse before she goes shopping may not only express love, it may bring her home sooner. Try new touches in new places and let your spouse give you feedback on whether he finds it pleasurable or not. Remember, he has the final word. You are learning to speak his language.

THE BODY IS FOR TOUCHING

Whatever there is of me resides in my body. To touch my body is to touch me. To withdraw from my body is to distance yourself from me emotionally. In our society, shaking hands is a way of communicating openness and social closeness to another individual. When on rare occasions one man refuses to shake hands with another, it communicates a message that things are not right in their relationship. All societies have some form of physical touching as a means of social greeting. The average American male may not feel comfortable with the European bear hug and kiss, but in Europe that serves the same function as our shaking hands.

There are appropriate and inappropriate ways to touch members of the opposite sex in every society. The recent attention to sexual harassment has highlighted the inappropriate ways. Within marriage, however, what is appropriate and inappropriate touching is determined by the couple themselves, within certain broad guidelines. Physical abuse is of course deemed inappropriate by society, and social organizations have been formed to help "the battered wife and the battered husband." Clearly our bodies are for touching, but not for abuse.

> If your spouse's primary love language is physical touch, nothing is more important than holding her as she cries.

This age is characterized as the age of sexual openness and freedom. With that freedom, we have demonstrated that the open marriage where both spouses are free to have sexual intimacies with other individuals is fanciful. Those who do not object on moral grounds eventually object on emotional grounds. Something about our need for intimacy and love does not allow us to give our spouse such freedom. The emotional pain is deep and intimacy evaporates when we are aware that our spouse is involved with someone else sexually. Counselors' files are filled with records of husbands and wives who are trying to grapple with the emotional trauma of an unfaithful spouse. That trauma, however, is compounded for the individual whose primary love language is physical touch. That for which he longs so deeply—love expressed by physical touch—is now being given to another. His emotional love tank is not only empty; it has been riddled by an explosion. It will take massive repairs for those emotional needs to be met.

CRISIS AND PHYSICAL TOUCH

Almost instinctively in a time of crisis, we hug one another. Why? Because physical touch is a powerful communicator of love. In a time of crisis, more than anything, we need to feel loved. We cannot always change events, but we can survive if we feel loved.

All marriages will experience crises. The death of parents is inevitable. Automobile accidents cripple and kill thousands each year. Disease is no respecter of persons. Disappointments are a part of life. The most important thing you can do for your mate in a time of crisis is to love him or her. If your spouse's primary love language is physical touch, nothing is more important than holding her as she cries. Your words may mean little, but your physical touch will communicate that you care. Crises provide a unique opportunity for expressing love. Your tender touches will be remembered long after the crisis has passed. Your failure to touch may never be forgotten.

"MARRIAGE IS NOT SUPPOSED TO BE THIS WAY"

Since my first visit to West Palm Beach, Florida, many years ago, I have always welcomed invitations to lead marriage seminars in that area. It was on one such occasion that I met Joe and Maria. They were not native to Florida (few are), but they had lived there for ten years and called West Palm Beach home. They had invited me to spend the night, and I knew from experience that such a request usually meant a late-night counseling session.

As the evening proceeded, I thoroughly enjoyed Joe and Maria's company. I found them to be a healthy, happily married couple. For a counselor, that is an oddity. I was eager to discover their secret, but being extremely tired and knowing that they were going to drive me to the airport the next day, I decided to do my probing when I was feeling more alert and we had forty-five minutes in the car together.

Maria and Joe began to tell me their story. In the early years of their marriage, they had tremendous difficulties. They had grown up in the same community, attended the same church, and graduated from the same high school. They liked the same music, the same sports, the same movies. They seemed to possess all the commonalities that are supposed to assure fewer conflicts in marriage.

They began dating in their senior year in high school. They attended separate colleges but saw each other frequently, and were married three weeks after he received his degree in business and she a degree in nursing. Two months later, they moved to Florida, where Joe had been offered a good job. The first three months were exciting—moving, finding a new apartment, enjoying life together.

They were about six months into the marriage when Maria began to feel that Joe was withdrawing from her. He was working longer hours, and when he was at home, he spent considerable time with the computer. When she finally expressed her feelings that he was avoiding her, Joe told her that he was not avoiding her but simply trying to stay on top of his job. He said that she didn't understand the pressure he was under and how important it was that he do well in his first year on the job. Maria wasn't pleased, but she decided to give him space.

She began to develop friendships with other wives who lived in the apartment complex. Often when she knew Joe was going to work late, she would go shopping with one of her friends instead of coming straight home after work. Sometimes she was not at home when Joe arrived. That annoyed him greatly, and he accused her of being thoughtless and irresponsible. Maria retorted, "Who's irresponsible? You don't even call me and let me know when you'll be home. How can I be here for you when I don't even know when you'll be here? And when you are here, you spend all your time working. You don't need a wife; all you need is a computer!"

To which Joe shot back, "I do need a wife. Don't you understand?

That's the whole point. I *do* need a wife."

But Maria did not understand. She was extremely confused. In her search for answers, she went to the public library and checked out several books on marriage. "Marriage is not supposed to be this way," she reasoned. "I have to find an answer to our situation." When Joe went on his laptop, Maria would pick up her book. In fact on many evenings, she read until midnight. On his way to bed, Joe would notice her and make sarcastic comments such as, "If you read that much in college, you would have made straight As." Maria would respond, "I'm not in college. I'm in marriage, and right now, I'd be satisfied with a C." Joe went to bed without so much as a second glance.

At the end of the first year, Maria was desperate. She had mentioned it before, but this time she calmly said to Joe, "I am going to find a marriage counselor. Do you want to go with me?"

But Joe answered, "I don't need a marriage counselor. I don't have time to go to a marriage counselor. I can't afford a marriage counselor."

"Then I'll go alone," said Maria.

"Fine, you're the one who needs counseling anyway."

The conversation was over. Maria felt totally alone, but the next week she made an appointment with a marriage therapist. After three sessions, the counselor called Joe and asked if he would be willing to come in to talk about his perspective on their marriage. Joe agreed, and the process of healing began. Six months later, they left the counselor's office with a new marriage.

I said to them, "What did you learn in counseling that turned your marriage around?"

"In essence, Dr. Chapman," Joe said, "we learned to speak each other's love language. The counselor did not use that term, but as you gave the lecture today, it came to me. My mind raced back to our counseling experience, and I realized that's exactly what happened to us. We finally learned to speak each other's love language."

"So what is your love language, Joe?" I asked.

"Physical touch," he said without hesitation.

"Physical touch for sure," said Maria.

"And yours, Maria?"

"Quality time, Dr. Chapman. That's what I was crying for in those days while he was spending all his time with his job and his computer."

"How did you learn that physical touch was Joe's love language?"

"It took awhile," Maria said. "Little by little, it began to come out in the counseling. At first, I don't think he even realized it."

> **"Once I waited for six weeks before she touched me at all."**

"It's true," Joe said. "I never told her that I wanted to be touched, although I was crying inside for her to reach out and touch me. In our dating relationship, I had always taken the initiative in touching, but she had always been responsive. I felt that she loved me, but after we got married, there were times that I reached out to her physically and . . . nothing. Maybe with her new job responsibilities, she was too tired. I don't know, but I took it personally. I felt that she didn't find me attractive. Then I decided I wouldn't even try because I didn't want to be rejected. So I waited to see how long it would be before she'd initiate a kiss or a touch or sexual intercourse. Once I waited for six weeks before she touched me at all. I couldn't stand it. My withdrawal was to stay away from the pain I felt when I was with her."

Then Maria said, "I had no idea that was what he was feeling. I knew that he was not reaching out to me. We weren't touching all the time like we did when we were dating, but I just assumed that since we were married, that was not as important to him now.

"I did go weeks without touching him. It didn't cross my mind. I was working, taking care of things at home, and trying to stay out of his way. I honestly didn't know what else I could be doing. I didn't understand why he wasn't paying attention to me. The thing is, spending time with me is what made me feel loved and appreciated. It really didn't matter whether we hugged or kissed. As long as he gave me his attention, I felt loved."

Once Joe and Maria discovered they were not meeting each other's need for love, they began to turn things around. "It was like I had a new husband," she said.

"What amazed me at the seminar today," Joe added, "was the way your lecture on love languages carried me back all these years to that experience. You said in twenty minutes what it took us six months to learn."

"Well," I said, "it's not how fast you learn it but how well you learn it that matters. And obviously, you have learned it well."

Joe is only one of many individuals for whom physical touch is the primary love language. Emotionally, they yearn for their spouse to reach out and touch them physically. Running the hand through the hair, giving a back rub, holding hands, embracing, sexual intercourse—all of those and other "love touches" are the emotional lifeline of the person for whom physical touch is the primary love language.

YOUR TURN

Recall some nonsexual "touching times" that enhanced intimacy between the two of you. What made these times special?

IF YOUR SPOUSE'S LOVE LANGUAGE IS
PHYSICAL TOUCH:

1. As you walk from the car to go shopping, reach out and hold your spouse's hand.

2. When you shop for your spouse, look for things that will appeal to their tactile nature—a cashmere sweater, a plush throw pillow, soft slippers.

3. Walk up to your spouse and say, "Have I told you lately that I love you?" Take her in your arms and hug her while you rub her back and continue. "You're the best!" Untangle yourself and move on to the next thing.

4. When you sit together in church, reach over and hold your spouse's hand during times of prayer.

5. Initiate sex by giving your spouse a foot massage. Continue to other parts of the body as long as it brings pleasure to your spouse.

6. When family or friends are visiting, touch your spouse in their presence. A hug, running your hand along his or her arm, putting your arm around him as you stand talking, or simply placing your hand on her shoulder can earn double emotional points. It says, "Even with all these people in our house, I still see you."

7. Couples separated by circumstances such as deployment use a variety of strategies to "touch" when they cannot be physically together, says author and former military wife Jocelyn Green. For example, a handwritten letter feels more tangible than an email. Some wives will wear an old shirt of their husband's around the house—one wife said, "I feel like he's hugging me when I wear his shirt." Sending a photo of yourself gives your spouse something of you to touch.

THE 5 love LANGUAGES®

Discovering Your Primary Love Language

Discovering the primary love language of your spouse is essential if you are to keep their emotional love tank full. But first, let's make sure you know your own love language. Having heard the five emotional love languages,

>	Words of Affirmation
>	Quality Time
>	Receiving Gifts
>	Acts of Service
>	Physical Touch,

some individuals will know instantaneously their own primary love language and that of their spouse. For others, it will not be that easy. Some are like Marcus, who said to me, "I don't know. It seems that two of those are just about equal for me."

"Which two?" I inquired.

"Physical touch and words of affirmation," he responded.

"By 'physical touch,' what do you mean?"

"Well, mainly sex," Marcus replied.

I probed a little further, asking, "Do you enjoy your wife running her hands through your hair, or giving you a back rub, or holding hands, or kissing and hugging you at times when you are not having sexual intercourse?"

"Sure," said Marcus. "I'm not going to turn them down, but the main thing is sex. That's when I know that she really loves me."

Leaving the subject of physical touch for a moment, I turned to affirming words and asked, "When you say that 'words of affirmation' are also important, what kinds of statements do you find most helpful?"

"I like it when she tells me I look good, that I'm smart—almost anything if it's positive. When she tells me she loves me!"

"Did you receive those kinds of comments from your parents when you were growing up?"

"Not very often," he said. "They yelled at me and told me what to do. But Alicia was different."

I asked Marcus to think about something. "Let me ask you this. If Alicia were meeting your sexual needs, that is, if you were having quality sexual intercourse as often as you desire, but she was giving you negative words, making critical remarks, sometimes putting you down in front of others, do you think you would feel loved by her?"

"No, not at all," he said. "I'd feel terrible."

"Marcus," I said, "I think we have just discovered that your primary love language is words of affirmation. Sexual intercourse is extremely important to you and to your sense of intimacy with Alicia, but her words of affirmation are more important to you emotionally. If she were, in fact, verbally critical of you all the time and put you down in front of other people, the time may come when you would no longer desire to have sexual intercourse with her because she would be a source of deep pain to you."

Marcus had made the mistake common to many men: assuming that physical touch is their primary love language because they desire sexual intercourse so intensely. For the male, sexual desire is physically based. That is, the desire for sexual intercourse is stimulated by the buildup of sperm cells and seminal fluid in the seminal vesicles. When the seminal vesicles are full, there is a physical push for release. Thus, the male's desire for sexual intercourse has a physical root.

For the female, sexual desire is far more influenced by her emotions. If she feels loved and admired and appreciated by her husband, then she has a desire to be physically intimate with him. But without the emotional closeness, she may have little physical desire. Her biological sexual drive is closely tied to her emotional need for love.

Because the male is physically pushed to have sexual release on a somewhat regular basis, he may automatically assume that that is his primary love language. But if he does not enjoy physical touch at other times and in nonsexual ways, it may not be his love language at all. Sexual desire is quite different from his emotional need to feel loved. That doesn't mean that sexual intercourse is unimportant to him—it is extremely important—but sexual intercourse alone will not meet his need to feel loved. His wife must speak his primary emotional love language as well.

When, in fact, his wife speaks his primary love

> **What do you most desire from your spouse? What makes you feel loved above all else?**

language and his emotional love tank is full, and he speaks her primary love language and her emotional tank is full, the sexual aspect of their relationship will take care of itself. Most sexual problems in marriage have little to do with physical technique but everything to do with meeting emotional needs.

After further conversation and reflection, Marcus said, "You know, I think you're right. Words of affirmation is definitely my primary love language. If she's critical and puts me down, I don't want to have sex with her and I even think about other women. But when she tells me how much she appreciates me and admires me . . . then it's a different story with us!"

Brittany has wondered for years whether she really has only one primary love language. "I know I most value quality time and acts of service," she said. "But it's hard to know which is primary with me. It used to be acts of service, but it seems that as I've gotten older I'm more concerned with sharing good times with friends and family and less worried about how stuff gets done."

> Each of the love languages is vulnerable to insincere manipulation.

How do you know?

HOW THE LOVE LANGUAGES CAN HURT US

What is your primary love language? What makes you feel most loved by your spouse? What do you desire above all else? If the answer to those questions does not leap to your mind immediately, perhaps it will help to look at the negative use of love languages. What does your spouse do or say—or fail to do or say—that hurts you deeply?

Ignoring our partner's love languages is like ignoring the needs of a garden: if we don't weed, water, or fertilize, it will die a slow death.

But if we actually abuse our partner's love languages—that is, use them for harmful purposes—it's like taking a machete to that same garden and chopping everything up.

Each of the love languages is vulnerable to insincere manipulation. The use of words your spouse loves to hear just so they will engage sexually with you is wrong. So is attempting to do a lot of chores for someone just so they will praise you.

If your deepest pain is the critical, judgmental words of your spouse, then perhaps your love language is words of affirmation. Sarcastic, hateful, or dismissive words are wounding to anyone, but especially so to the person for whom affirming words is their love language.

Similarly, the *lack* of words—giving someone the "silent treatment"—can be devastating.

We have already discussed the hurt and anger felt by spouses who resent their mates for "not helping enough" around the house. Clearly these spouses' love language is acts of service. But recently I heard about a wife who took this a step further. She and her husband had been arguing all weekend. On Sunday, rather than make lunch for the two of them as usual, she fixed something for herself and told him, "Make your own lunch." She withdrew a service she had always performed for him—knowing his love language was acts of service.

If your primary love language is gifts, you may relate to the story of the young girl who had a very hard Christmas one year. Her older brother had not spent much time or effort on his gift giving. He gave her something he had found lying around the house—nothing she needed, nothing special or thoughtful. She, of course, was deeply wounded.

But at least as destructive, as we saw with Sonia and her softball-playing husband, Tony, is withholding the gift of yourself—your presence.

Similarly, the spouse whose love language is quality time might find herself more bored by her and her husband's evening routine of dinner, TV, and bed, or struggle more when her spouse travels on business. She might even long for more meaningful emails than "Good meeting today—see you tomorrow."

What of physical touch? Touch, of course, has immense potential for abuse, as we have already discussed. Touch can comfort, reassure, encourage, invite; it can also scar physically and emotionally. Touch withheld can also bring pain.

WHAT ARE YOU ASKING?

When you're trying to figure out your primary love language, it helps to look back over your marriage and ask, "What have I most often requested of my spouse?" Whatever you have most requested is probably in keeping with your primary love language. Those requests have probably been interpreted by your spouse as nagging—but in fact, they have been your efforts to secure emotional love from your spouse.

Brittany, the woman who was wondering if she was more quality time or acts of service, has thought about this. "I guess by this measure I do lean more toward service, if only because I feel like I'm always asking my husband to do stuff."

Another way to discover your primary love language is to examine what you do or say to express love to your spouse. Chances are what you are doing for her is what you wish she would do for you. If you are constantly doing acts of service for your spouse, perhaps (although not always) that is your love language. If words of affirmation speak love to you, chances are you will use them in speaking love to your spouse. Thus, you may discover your own language by asking, "How do I consciously express my love to my spouse?"

But remember, that approach is only a possible clue to your love language; it is not an absolute indicator. For example, the husband who learned from his father to express love to his wife by giving her nice gifts expresses his love to his wife by doing what his father did, yet receiving gifts is not his primary love language. He is simply doing what he was trained to do by his father.

> **Your picture of a perfect mate should give you some idea of your primary love language.**

I have suggested three ways to discover your own primary love language:

1. What does your spouse do or fail to do that hurts you most deeply? The opposite of what hurts you most is probably your love language.

2. What have you most often requested of your spouse? The thing you have most often requested is likely the thing that would make you feel most loved.

3. In what way do you regularly express love to your spouse? Your method of expressing love may be an indication that that would also make you feel loved.

Using those three approaches will probably enable you to determine your primary love language. If two languages seem to be equal for you, that is, both speak loudly to you, then perhaps you are bilingual. If so, you make it easier on your spouse. Now he or she has two choices, either of which will strongly communicate love to you.

You may also wish to take the 5 Love Languages Profile found at the back of the book. Discuss the results with your spouse.

Two kinds of people may have difficulty discovering their primary love language. The first is the individual whose emotional love tank has been full for a long time. Her spouse has expressed love in many ways, and she is not certain which of those ways makes her feel most loved. She simply knows that she is loved. The second is the individual whose love tank has been empty for so long that he doesn't remember what makes him feel loved. In either case, go back to the experience of falling in love and ask yourself, "What did I like about my spouse in those days? What did he do or say that made me desire to be with him?" If you can conjure up those memories, it will give you some idea of your primary love language. You could also ask yourself, "What would be an ideal spouse to me? If I could have the perfect mate, what would she be like?" Your picture of a perfect mate should give you some idea of your primary love language.

Having said all of that, let me suggest that you spend some time writing down what you think is your primary love language. Then list the other four in order of importance. Also write down what you think is the primary love language of your spouse. You may also list the other four in order of importance if you wish. Sit down with your spouse and discuss what you guessed to be his/her primary love language. Then tell each other what you consider to be your own primary love language.

Once you have shared that information, I suggest that you play the following game three times a week for three weeks. The game is called "Tank Check," and it is played like this. When you come home, one of you says to the other, "On a scale of zero to ten, how is your love tank tonight?" Zero means empty, and 10 means "I am full of love and can't handle any more." You give a reading on your emotional love tank—10, 9, 8, 7, 6, 5, 4, 3, 2, 1, or 0, indicating how full it is. Your spouse says, "What could I do to help fill it?"

Then you make a suggestion—something you would like your spouse to do or say that evening. To the best of his ability, he will respond to your request. Then you repeat the process in the reverse order so that both of you have the opportunity to do a reading on your love tank and to make a suggestion toward filling it. If you play the game for three weeks, you will be hooked on it, and it can be a playful way of stimulating love expressions in your marriage.

One husband said to me, "I don't like that love tank game. I played it with my wife. I came home and said to her, 'On a scale of zero to ten, how's your love tank tonight?' She said, 'About seven.' I asked, 'What could I do to help fill it?' She said, 'The greatest thing you could do for me tonight is to do the laundry.' I said, 'Love and laundry? I don't get it.'"

I said, "That's the problem. Perhaps you don't understand your wife's love language. What's your primary love language?"

Without hesitation he said, "Physical touch, and especially the sexual part of the marriage."

"Listen to me carefully," I said. "The love you feel when your wife expresses love by physical touch is the same love your wife feels when you do the laundry."

"Bring on the laundry!" he shouted. "I'll wash the clothes every night if it makes her feel that good."

Incidentally, if you have still not discovered your primary love language, keep records on the tank check game. When your spouse says, "What could I do to help fill your tank?" your suggestions will likely cluster around your primary love language. You may request things from all five love languages, but you will have more requests centering on your primary love language.

Perhaps some of you are saying in your minds what one couple said to me in Zion, Illinois. "Dr. Chapman, all that sounds fine and wonderful, but what if the love language of your spouse is something that just doesn't come naturally for you?"

I'll discuss my answer in chapter 10.

YOUR TURN

Do you think by now you have a good sense of what your spouse's love language is? How about them for you? What more could you do to explore this?

If your love tank is completely empty or very full, whether you know your love language or not, play the Tank Check game over the next month. Ask for a reading from 0 to 10 three evenings a week, and then take the suggestions of your spouse to raise that number for him/her. If your spouse is at a 10 consistently, you can pat yourself on the back—but don't stop loving.

THE 5 *love* LANGUAGES®

10

Love Is a Choice

How can we speak each other's love language when we are full of hurt, anger, and resentment over past failures? The answer to that question lies in the essential nature of our humanity. We are creatures of choice. That means that we have the capacity to make poor choices, which all of us have done. We have spoken critical words, and we have done hurtful things. We are not proud of those choices, although they may have seemed justified at the moment. Poor choices in the past don't mean that we must make them in the future. Instead we can say, "I'm sorry. I know I have hurt you, but I would like to make the future different. I would like to love you in your language. I would like to meet your needs." I have seen marriages rescued from the brink of divorce when couples make the choice to love.

Love doesn't erase the past, but it makes the future different. When we choose active expressions of love in the primary love language of our spouse, we create an emotional climate where we can deal with our past conflicts and failures.

"I JUST DON'T LOVE HER ANYMORE"

Brent was in my office, stone-faced and seemingly unfeeling. He had come not by his own initiative but at my request. A week earlier his wife, Becky, had been sitting in the same chair, crying. Between her outbursts of tears, she managed to verbalize that Brent had told her that he no longer loved her and that he was leaving. She was devastated.

When she regained her composure, she said, "We have both worked so hard the last two or three years. I knew that we were not spending as much time together as we used to, but I thought we were working for a common goal. I cannot believe what he is saying. He has always been such a kind and caring person. He is such a good father to our children." She continued, "How could he do this to us?"

I listened as she described their twelve years of marriage. It was a story I had heard many times before. They had an exciting courtship, got married at the height of the "in-love" experience, had the typical adjustments in the early days of marriage, and pursued the American dream. In due time, they came down off the emotional high of the "in-love" experience but did not learn to speak each other's love language sufficiently. She had lived with a love tank only half full for the last several years, but she had received enough expressions of love to make her think that everything was okay. However, his love tank was empty.

I told Becky that I would see if Brent would talk with me. I told Brent on the phone, "As you know, Becky came to see me and told me about her struggle with what is happening in the marriage. I want to help her, but in order to do so, I need to know what you are thinking."

He agreed readily, and now he sat in my office. His outward appearance was in stark contrast to Becky's. She had been weeping uncontrollably, but he was stoic. I had the impression, however, that his weeping had taken place weeks or perhaps months ago and that it had been an inward weeping. The story Brent told confirmed my hunch.

"I just don't love her anymore," he said. "I haven't loved her for a long time. I don't want to hurt her, but we are not close. Our relationship has become empty. I don't enjoy being with her anymore. I don't know what happened. I wish it were different, but I don't have any feelings for her."

Brent was thinking and feeling what hundreds of thousands of husbands have thought and felt through the years. It's the "I don't love her anymore" mindset that gives men the emotional freedom to seek love with someone else. The same is true for wives who use the same excuse.

I sympathized with Brent, for I have been there. Thousands of husbands and wives have been there—emotionally empty, wanting to do the right thing, not wanting to hurt anyone, but being pushed by their emotional needs to seek love outside the marriage. Fortunately, I had discovered in the earlier years of my own marriage the difference between the "in-love" experience and the "emotional need" to feel loved. Most in our society have not yet learned that difference.

The "in-love" experience that we discussed in chapter 3 is on the level of instinct. It is not premeditated; it simply happens in the normal context of male-female relationships. It can be fostered or quenched, but it does not arise by conscious choice. It is short-lived (usually two years or less) and seems to serve for humankind the same function as the mating call of the Canada goose.

The "in-love" experience temporarily meets one's emotional need for love. It gives us the feeling that someone cares, that someone admires us and appreciates us. Our emotions soar with the thought that another person sees us as number one, that he or she is willing to devote time and energies exclusively to our relationship. For a brief period, however long it lasts, our emotional need for love is met. Our tank is full; we can conquer the world. Nothing is impossible. For many individuals, it is the first time they have ever lived with a full emotional tank, and it is euphoric.

In time, however, we come down from that natural high back to the real world. If our spouse has learned to speak our primary love language, our need for love will continue to be satisfied. If, on the other hand, he or she does not speak our love language, our tank will slowly drain, and we will no longer feel loved. Meeting that need in one's spouse is definitely a choice. If I learn the emotional love language of my spouse and speak it frequently, she will continue to feel loved. When she comes down from the obsession of the "in-love" experience, she will hardly even miss it because her emotional love tank will continue to be filled. However, if I have not learned her primary love language or have chosen not to speak it, when she descends from the emotional high, she will have the natural yearnings of unmet emotional needs. After some years of living with an empty love tank, she will likely "fall in love" with someone else, and the cycle will begin again.

> **I looked at Brent and knew in my heart that he was probably already involved with another "in-love" experience.**

Meeting my wife's need for love is a choice I make each day. If I know her primary love language and choose to speak it, her deepest emotional needs will be met, and she will feel secure in my love. If she does the same for me, my emotional needs are met and both of us live with a full tank. In a state of emotional contentment, both of us will give our creative energies to many wholesome projects outside the marriage while we continue to keep our marriage exciting and growing.

With all of that in my mind, I looked back at the deadpan face of Brent and wondered if I could help him. I knew in my heart that he was probably already involved with another "in-love" experience. I wondered if it was in the beginning stages or at its height. Few men who suffer from an empty emotional love tank leave their marriage until they have prospects of meeting that need somewhere else.

Brent was honest and revealed that he had been in love with someone else for several months. He had hoped that the feelings would go away and that he could work things out with his wife. But things at home had gotten worse, and his love for the other woman had increased. He could not imagine living without his new lover.

I sympathized with Brent in his dilemma. He sincerely did not want to hurt his wife or his children, but at the same time, he felt he deserved a life of happiness. I told him the statistics: that the divorce rate is higher in second marriages. He was surprised to hear that but was certain that he would beat the odds. I told him about the research on the effects of divorce on children, but he was convinced that he would continue to be a good father to his children and that they would get over the trauma of the divorce. I talked to Brent about the issues in this book and explained the difference between the experience of falling in love and the deep emotional need to feel loved. I explained the five love languages and challenged him to give his marriage another chance. All the while, I knew that my intellectual and reasoned approach to marriage compared to the emotional high that he was experiencing was like pitting a BB gun against an automatic weapon. He expressed appreciation for my concern and asked that I do everything possible to help Becky. But he assured me that he saw no hope for the marriage.

COMING DOWN OFF THE HIGH

One month later, I received a call from Brent. He indicated that he would like to talk with me again. This time when he entered my office, he was noticeably disturbed. He was not the calm, cool man I had seen before. His lover had begun to come down off the emotional high, and she was observing things in Brent that she did not like. She was withdrawing from the relationship, and he was crushed. Tears came to his eyes as he told me how much she meant to him and how unbearable it was to experience her rejection.

I listened for an hour before Brent ever asked for my advice. I told him how sympathetic I was to his pain and indicated that what he was experiencing was the natural emotional grief from a loss, and that the grief would not go away overnight. I explained, however, that the experience was inevitable. I reminded him of the temporary nature of the "in-love" experience, that sooner or later, we always come down from the high to the real world. Some fall out of love before they get married; others, after they get married. He agreed that it was better now than later.

After a while, I suggested that perhaps the crisis was a good time for him and his wife to get some marriage counseling. I reminded him that true, long-lasting emotional love is a choice and that emotional love could be reborn in his marriage if he and his wife learned to love each other in the right love languages. He agreed to marriage counseling, and nine months later, Brent and Becky left my office with a reborn marriage. When I saw Brent three years later, he told me what a wonderful marriage he had and thanked me for helping him at a crucial time in his life. He told me that the grief over losing the other lover had been gone for more than two years. He smiled and said, "My tank has never been so full, and Becky is the happiest woman you are ever going to meet."

Fortunately Brent was the benefactor of what I call the disequilibrium of the "in-love" experience. That is, almost never do two people fall in love on the same day, and almost never do they fall out of love on the same day. You don't have to be a social scientist to discover that truth. Just listen to country music. Brent's lover happened to have fallen out of love at an opportune time.

THE POWER OF CHOOSING TO LOVE

In the nine months that I counseled Brent and Becky, we worked through numerous conflicts that they had never resolved before. But the key to the rebirth of their marriage was discovering each other's primary love language and choosing to speak it frequently.

Let me return to the question I raised in chapter 9. "What if the love language of your spouse is something that doesn't come naturally for you?" I am often asked this question at my marriage seminars, and my answer is always, "So?"

My wife's love language is acts of service. One of the things I do for her regularly as an act of love is to vacuum the floors. Do you think that vacuuming floors comes naturally for me? My mother used to make me vacuum. All through

> **Most of us do many things each day that do not come "naturally" for us.**

junior high and high school, I couldn't go play ball on Saturday until I finished vacuuming the entire house. In those days, I said to myself, "When I get out of here, one thing I am not going to do: I am not going to vacuum houses. I'll get myself a wife to do that."

But I vacuum our house now, and I vacuum it regularly. There is only one reason I vacuum our house. Love. You couldn't pay me enough to vacuum a house, but I do it for love. You see, when an action doesn't come naturally to you, it is a greater expression of love. My wife knows that when I vacuum the house, it's nothing but 100 percent pure, unadulterated love, and I get credit for the whole thing!

Someone says, "But, Dr. Chapman, that's different. I know that my spouse's love language is physical touch, and I am not a toucher. I never saw my mother and father hug each other. They never hugged me. I am just not a toucher. What am I going to do?"

Do you have two hands? Can you put them together? Now, imagine that you have your spouse in the middle and pull him/her toward you. I'll bet that if you hug your spouse three thousand times, it will begin to feel more comfortable. But ultimately, comfort is not the issue. We are talking about love, and love is something you do for someone else, not something you do for yourself. Most of us do many things each day that do not come "naturally" for us. For some of us, that is getting out of bed in the morning. We go against our feelings and get out of bed. Why? Because we believe there is something worthwhile to do that day. And normally, before the day is over, we feel good about having gotten up. Our actions preceded our emotions.

The same is true with love. We discover the primary love language of our spouse, and we choose to speak it whether or not it is natural for us. We are not claiming to have warm, excited feelings. We are simply choosing to do it for his or her benefit. We want to meet our spouse's emotional needs, and we reach out to speak his love language. In so doing, his emotional love tank is filled and chances are he will reciprocate and speak our language. When he does, our emotions return, and our love tank begins to fill.

Love is a choice. And either partner can start the process today.

YOUR TURN

A key thought here is the idea of speaking our mate's love language whether or not it is natural for us. Why is this so fundamental to a healthy marriage?

THE 5 love LANGUAGES®

11

Love Makes the Difference

Love is not our only emotional need. Psychologists have observed that among our basic needs are the need for security, self-worth, and significance. Love, however, interfaces with all of those.

If I feel loved by my spouse, I can relax, knowing that my lover will do me no ill. I feel secure in her presence. I may face many uncertainties in my vocation. I may have enemies in other areas of my life, but with my spouse I feel secure.

My sense of self-worth is fed by the fact that my spouse loves me. After all, if she loves me, I must be worth loving. My parents may have given me negative or mixed messages about my worth, but my spouse knows me as an adult and loves me. Her love builds my self-esteem.

The need for significance is the emotional force behind much of our behavior. Life is driven by the desire for success. We want our lives to count for something. We have our own idea of what it means to be significant, and we work hard to reach our goals. Feeling loved by a spouse enhances our sense of significance. We reason, *If someone loves me, I must have significance.*

I am significant because I stand at the apex of the created order. I have the ability to think in abstract terms, communicate my thoughts via words, and make decisions. By means of printed or recorded words, I can benefit from the thoughts of those who have preceded me. I can profit from others' experiences, though they lived in a different age and culture. I experience the death of family and friends and sense that there is existence beyond the material. I discover that, in all cultures, people believe in a spiritual world. My heart tells me it is true even when my mind, trained in scientific observation, raises critical questions.

> **True love always liberates.**

I am significant. Life has meaning. There is a higher purpose. I want to believe it, but I may not feel significant until someone expresses love to me. When my spouse lovingly invests time, energy, and effort in me, I believe that I am significant. Without love, I may spend a lifetime in search of significance, self-worth, and security. When I experience love, it influences all of those needs positively. I am now freed to develop my potential. I am more secure in my self-worth and can now turn my efforts outward instead of being obsessed with my own needs. True love always liberates.

In the context of marriage, if we do not feel loved, our differences are magnified. We come to view each other as a threat to our happiness. We fight for self-worth and significance, and marriage becomes a battlefield rather than a haven.

Love is not the answer to everything, but it creates a climate of security in which we can seek answers to those things that bother us.

In the security of love, a couple can discuss differences without condemnation. Conflicts can be resolved. Two people who are different can learn to live together in harmony. We discover how to bring out the best in each other. Those are the rewards of love.

"WE'RE LIKE ROOMMATES"

When John and Susan arrived at my office, they had been traveling for three hours. It was obvious John did not want to be there. Susan had twisted his arm by threats of leaving him. (I do not suggest this approach, but people do not always know my suggestions before they come to see me.) They had been married for more than thirty years and had never gone to counseling before.

Susan began the conversation. "Dr. Chapman, I want you to know two things up front. First of all, we don't have any money problems. I was reading in a magazine that money is the biggest problem in marriage. That's not true for us. We both have worked through the years, the house is paid for, the cars are paid for. Second, I want you to know that we don't argue. I hear my friends talking about the arguments they have all the time. I can't remember the last time we ever had an argument. Both of us agree that arguing is fruitless, so we don't argue."

As a counselor, I appreciated Susan's clearing the path. I knew that she was going to get right to the point.

She continued. "The problem is that I just don't feel any love coming from my husband. Life is a routine for us. We get up in the morning and go off to work. In the afternoon, he does his thing and I do my thing. We generally have dinner together, but we don't talk. He watches TV while we eat. After dinner, he putters in the basement and then sleeps in front of the TV until I tell him it's time to go to bed. That's our schedule five days a week. On Saturday, he plays golf in the morning, works in the yard in the afternoon, and we go out to dinner with another couple on Saturday night. He talks to them, but when we get into the car to go home, the conversation is over. On Sunday morning, we go to church. And so on.

"We're like two roommates living in the same house. There is nothing going on between us. I don't feel any love coming from him. There's no warmth, there's no emotion. It's empty; it's dead. I don't think I can go on much longer like this."

By that time, Susan was crying. I handed her a tissue and looked at John. His first comment was, "I don't understand her." After a brief pause, he continued. "I have done everything I know to show her that I love her, especially the last two or three years since she's been complaining about it so much. Nothing seems to help. No matter what I do, she continues to complain that she doesn't feel loved. I don't know what else to do."

I could tell that John was frustrated and exasperated. I inquired, "What have you been doing to show your love for Susan?"

"Well, for one thing," he said, "I get home from work before she does, so I get dinner started every night. In fact, if you want to know the truth, I have dinner almost ready when she gets home four nights a week. The other night, we go out to eat. I do all the vacuuming because her back is bad. I do all the yard work because she is allergic to pollen. I fold the clothes when they come out of the dryer."

He went on telling me other things that he did for Susan. When he finished, I wondered, *What does this woman do?*

John continued, "I do all those things to show her that I love her, yet she sits there and says to you what she

> "I want him to talk to me about us, about our lives."

has been saying to me for two or three years—that she doesn't feel loved. I don't know what else to do for her."

When I turned back to Susan, she said, "Dr. Chapman, all of those things are fine, but I want him to sit and talk to me. We don't ever talk. He's always doing something. I want him to be with me, give me some time, look at me, talk to me about us, about our lives."

Susan was crying again. It was obvious to me that her primary love language was quality time. She was crying for attention. She wanted to be treated as a person, not an object. John's busyness did not meet her emotional needs. As I talked further with John, I discovered that he didn't feel loved either, but he wasn't talking about it. He reasoned, "If you have been married for thirty-five years and your bills are paid and you don't argue, what more can you hope for?" That's where he was. But when I said to him, "What would be an ideal wife to you? If you could have a perfect wife, what would she be like?" he looked me in the eye for the first time and asked, "Do you really want to know?"

"Yes," I said.

He sat up on the couch and folded his arms across his chest. A big smile broke on his face, and he said, "I've dreamed about this. A perfect wife would be a wife who would come home in the afternoon and fix dinner for me. I would be working in the yard, and she would call me in to eat. After dinner, she would wash the dishes. I would probably help her some, but she would take the responsibility. She would sew the buttons on my shirt when they fall off."

Susan could contain herself no longer. She turned to him and said, "But you told me that you liked to cook."

"I don't mind cooking," John responded, "but the man asked me what would be ideal."

I knew John's primary love language without another word—acts of service. In his mind, that was the way you show love: by doing things for people. The problem was that "doing things" was not Susan's primary love language. It did not mean to her emotionally what it would have meant to him if she had been doing things for him.

When the truth dawned on John, the first thing he said was, "Why didn't somebody tell me this years ago? I could have been sitting talking to her fifteen minutes every night instead of doing all this stuff."

He turned to Susan and said, "For the first time in my life, I finally understand what you mean when you say 'We don't talk.' I could never understand that. I thought we did talk. I always ask, 'Did you sleep well?' I thought we were talking, but now I understand. I'll give you fifteen minutes every night for the rest of my life—starting tonight. You can count on that."

Susan looked at John. "I would love that. And," she continued, "I don't mind fixing dinner for you. It will have to be later than usual because I get off work later than you, but I don't mind cooking. And I'll be happy to sew your buttons on. You never left them off long enough for me to get them. I'll wash dishes the rest of my life if it will make you feel loved."

Susan and John went home and started loving each other in the right love languages. In less than two months, they were on a second honeymoon. After a trip to the Bahamas, they called to tell me what a radical change had taken place in their marriage.

Can emotional love be reborn in a marriage? You bet. The key is to learn the primary love language of your spouse and choose to speak it.

YOUR TURN

What does your spouse do to make you feel more "significant"? How about what you do for them?

THE **5 *love*** LANGUAGES®

12

Loving the Unlovely

It was a beautiful September Saturday. My wife and I were strolling through Reynolda Gardens, enjoying the flora, some of which had been imported from around the world. The gardens had originally been developed by R. J. Reynolds, the tobacco magnate, as a part of his country estate. They are now a part of the Wake Forest University campus. We had just passed the rose garden when I noticed Ann, a woman who had begun counseling two weeks earlier, approaching us. She was looking down at the cobblestone walkway and appeared to be in deep thought. When I greeted her, she was startled but looked up and smiled. I introduced her to Karolyn, and we exchanged pleasantries. Then, without any lead-in, she asked me one of the most profound questions I have ever heard: "Dr. Chapman, is it possible to love someone whom you hate?"

I knew the question was born of deep hurt and deserved a thoughtful answer. I knew that I would be seeing her the following week for another counseling appointment, so I said, "Ann, that is one of the most thought-provoking questions I have ever heard. Why don't we discuss that next week?" She agreed, and Karolyn and I continued our stroll. But Ann's question did not go away. Later, as we drove home, Karolyn and I discussed it. We reflected on the early days of our own marriage and remembered that we had often experienced feelings of hate. Our condemning words to each other had brought us hurt and, on the heels of hurt, anger. And anger held inside becomes hate.

What made the difference for us? We both knew it was the choice to love. We had realized that if we continued our pattern of demanding and condemning, we would destroy our marriage. Fortunately over a period of about a year, we had learned how to discuss our differences without condemning each other, how to make decisions without destroying our unity, how to give constructive suggestions without being demanding, and eventually how to speak each other's primary love language. Our choice to love was made in the midst of negative feelings toward each other. When we started speaking each other's primary love language, the feelings of anger and hate abated.

> **Is it possible to love a spouse who has become your enemy?**

Our situation, however, was different from Ann's. Karolyn and I had both been open to learning and growing. I knew that Ann's husband was not. She had told me the previous week that she had begged him to go for counseling. She had pleaded for him to read a book or listen to a speaker on marriage, but he had refused all her efforts toward growth. According to her, his attitude was: "I don't have any problems. You are the one with the problems." In his mind he was right; she was wrong—it was as simple as that. Her feelings of love for him had been killed through the years by his constant criticism and condemnation. After ten years of marriage, her emotional energy was depleted and her self-esteem almost destroyed. Was there hope for Ann's marriage? Could she love an unlovely husband? Would he ever respond in love to her?

LOVE'S GREATEST CHALLENGE

I knew that Ann was a deeply religious person and that she attended church regularly. I surmised that perhaps her only hope for marital survival was in her faith. The next day, with Ann in mind, I began to read Luke's account of the life of Christ. I have always admired Luke's writing because he was a physician who gave attention to details and in the first century wrote an orderly account of the teachings and lifestyle of Jesus of Nazareth. In what many have called Jesus' greatest sermon, I read the following words, which I call love's greatest challenge.

> But to you who are listening I say: Love your enemies, do good to those who hate you, bless those who curse you, pray for those who mistreat you. . . . Do to others as you would have them do to you. If you love those who love you, what credit is that to you? Even sinners love those who love them.[3]

It seemed to me that that profound challenge, written almost two thousand years ago, might be the direction that Ann was looking for, but could she do it? Could anyone do it? Is it possible to love a spouse who has become your enemy? Is it possible to love one who has cursed you, mistreated you, and expressed feelings of contempt and hate for you? And if she could, would there be any payback? Would her husband ever change and begin to express love and care for her? I was astounded by this further word from Jesus' sermon: "Give, and it will be given to you. A good measure, pressed down, shaken together and running over, will be poured into your lap. For with the measure you use, it will be measured to you."[4]

Could that principle of loving an unlovely person possibly work in a marriage as far gone as Ann's? I decided to do an experiment. I would take as my hypothesis that if Ann could learn her husband's primary love language and speak it for a period of time so that his emotional need for love was met, eventually he would reciprocate and begin to express love to her. I wondered, *Would it work?*

I met with Ann the next week and listened again as she reviewed the hurts in her marriage. At the end of her synopsis, she repeated the question she had asked in Reynolda Gardens. This time she put it in the form of a statement: "Dr. Chapman, I just don't know if I can ever love him again after all he has done to me."

"Have you talked about your situation with any of your friends?" I asked.

"With two of my closest friends," she said, "and a little bit with some other people."

"And what was their response?"

"'Get out,'" she said. "They all tell me to get out, that he will never change, and that I am simply prolonging the agony. But I just can't bring myself to do that. Maybe I should, but I just can't believe that's the right thing to do."

"It seems to me that you are torn between your religious and moral beliefs that tell you it is wrong to get out of the marriage, and your emotional pain, which tells you that getting out is the only way to survive," I said.

"That's exactly right, Dr. Chapman. That's exactly the way I feel. I don't know what to do."

"I am deeply sympathetic with your struggle," I continued. "You are in a very difficult situation. I wish I could offer you an easy answer. Unfortunately, I can't. Both of the alternatives you mentioned, getting out or staying in, will likely bring you a great deal of pain. Before you make that decision, I do have one idea. I am not sure it will work, but I'd like you to try it. I know from what you have told me that your religious faith is important to you and that you have a great deal of respect for the teachings of Jesus."

She nodded. I continued, "I want to read something that Jesus once said that I think has some application to your marriage." I read slowly and deliberately.

> "'But to you who are listening I say: Love your enemies, do good to those who hate you, bless those who curse you, pray for those who mistreat you.... Do to others as you would have them do to you. If you love those who love you, what credit is that to you? Even sinners love those who love them.'"

"Does that sound like your husband? Has he treated you as an enemy rather than as a friend?"

She paused. "Yes," she said quietly.

"Has he ever cursed you?" I asked.

"Many times."

"Has he ever mistreated you?"

"Often."

"And has he told you that he hates you?"

"Yes."

THE SIX-MONTH EXPERIMENT

"Ann, if you are willing, I would like to do an experiment. I would like to see what would happen if we apply this principle to your marriage. Let me explain what I mean." I went on to explain to Ann the concept of the emotional tank and the fact that when the tank is low, as hers was, we have no love feelings toward our spouse but simply experience emptiness and pain. I told her that if we could learn to speak each other's primary love language, that emotional need could be met and positive feelings could grow again.

"Does that make sense to you?" I inquired.

"Dr. Chapman, you have just described my life. I have never seen it so clearly before. We were in love before we got married, but not long after our marriage, we came down off the high and we never learned to speak each other's love language. My tank has been empty for years, and I am sure his has also. Dr. Chapman, if I had understood this concept earlier, maybe none of this would have happened."

"We can't go back, Ann," I said. "All we can do is try to make the future different. I would like to propose a six-month experiment."

"I'll try anything," Ann said.

I liked her positive spirit, but I wasn't sure whether she understood how difficult the experiment would be.

"Let's begin by stating our objective," I said. "If in six months you could have your fondest wish, what would it be?"

Ann sat in silence for some time. Then thoughtfully she said, "I would like to see us doing things together, going places together. I would like to feel that he is interested in my world. I'd like him to listen to me. I'd like to feel that he values my ideas. I would like to see us taking trips together and having fun again. I would like to know that he values our marriage more than anything."

Ann paused and then continued. "On my part, I would like to have warm, positive feelings toward him again. I would like to gain respect for him again. I would like to be proud of him. Right now, I don't have those feelings."

I was writing as Ann was speaking. When she finished, I read aloud what she had said. "That sounds like a pretty lofty objective," I said, "but is that really what you want, Ann?"

"More than anything."

"Then let's agree," I said, "that this will be our objective. In six months, we want to see you and Glenn having this kind of love relationship.

"Now, let me suggest a hypothesis. Let's hypothesize that if you could speak Glenn's primary love language consistently for a six-month period, that somewhere along the line his emotional need for love would begin to be met; and as his emotional tank filled, he would begin to reciprocate love to you."

I continued, "You understand that this places all the initiative in your hands. Glenn is not trying to work on this marriage. You are. But if you can channel your energies in the right direction, there is a good possibility that Glenn will eventually reciprocate." I read the other portion of Jesus' sermon recorded by Luke, the physician. *"Give, and it will be given to you. A good measure, pressed down, shaken together and running over, will be poured into your lap. For with the measure you use, it will be measured to you."*

"Generally speaking, if we are kind and loving toward people, they will tend to be kind and loving toward us. That does not mean that we can *make* a person kind by being kind to him. We are independent agents. Thus, we can spurn love and walk away from love or even spit into the face of love. There is no guarantee that Glenn will respond to your acts of love. We can only say that there is a good possibility he will do so."

"I WANT TO BE A BETTER WIFE TO YOU"

We then discussed Ann and Glenn's primary love languages. I guessed hers was quality time, and Ann confirmed it. "In our early days we spent long hours talking together, doing things together. I really felt loved. More than anything, I wish that part of our marriage could return. When we spend time together, I feel like he really cares, but when he's always doing other things, I feel like business and other pursuits are more important than our relationship."

"And what do you think Glenn's primary love language is?" I inquired.

"I think it is physical touch, and especially the sexual part of the marriage. I know that when I felt more loved by him and we were more sexually active, he had a different attitude. I think that's his primary love language."

"Does he ever complain about the way you talk to him?"

"Well, he says I nag him all the time. He also says that I don't support him, that I'm always against his ideas."

"Then let's assume," I said, "that physical touch is his primary love language and words of affirmation is his secondary love language. The reason I suggest the second is that if he complains about negative words, apparently positive words would be meaningful to him.

"Now what if you go home and say to Glenn, 'I've been thinking about us and I've decided that I would like to be a better wife to you. So if you have any suggestions, I want you to know that I am open to them. You can tell me now or you can think about it and let me know what you think, but I would really like to work on this.' Whatever his response, negative or positive, simply accept it as information. That initial statement lets him know that something different is about to happen in your relationship.

"Then based upon your guess that his primary love language is physical touch and my suggestion that his secondary love language may be words of affirmation, focus your attention on those two areas for one month.

"If Glenn comes back with a suggestion as to how you might be a better wife, accept that information and work it into your plan. Look for positive things in Glenn's life and give him verbal affirmation about those things. In the meantime, stop all verbal complaints. If you want to complain about something, write it down in your personal notebook rather than saying anything about it to Glenn this month.

> "You will probably have to rely heavily on your faith in God in order to do this."

"Begin taking more initiative in physical touch and sexual involvement. Surprise him by being aggressive, not simply responding to his advances. Set a goal to have sexual intercourse at least once a week the first two weeks and twice a week the following two weeks." Ann had told me that she and Glenn had had sexual intercourse only once or twice in the past six months. I figured this plan would get things off dead center rather quickly.

"Oh, Dr. Chapman, this is going to be difficult," Ann said. "I have found it hard to be sexually responsive to him when he ignores me all the time. I have felt used rather than loved in our sexual encounters. He acts as though I am totally unimportant all the rest of the time, and then he wants to jump in bed and use my body."

"Your response has been natural and normal," I assured Ann. "Usually if a wife feels loved by her husband, she will desire sexual intimacy. If she does not, she will likely feel used in the sexual context. That is why loving someone who is not loving you is extremely difficult. It goes against our natural tendencies. You will probably have to rely heavily upon your faith in God in order to do this. Perhaps it will help if you read again Jesus' sermon on loving your enemies, loving those who hate you, loving those who use you. And then ask God to help you practice the teachings of Jesus."

I could tell that Ann was following what I was saying. Her head was nodding ever so slightly. Her eyes told me she had lots of questions.

"But, Dr. Chapman, isn't it being hypocritical to express love sexually when you have such negative feelings toward the person?"

"Perhaps it would be helpful for us to distinguish between love as a feeling and love as an action," I said. "If you claim to have feelings that you do not have, that is hypocritical and such false communication is not the way to build intimate relationships. But if you express an act of love that is designed for the other person's benefit or pleasure, it is simply a choice. You are not claiming that the action grows out of a deep emotional bonding. You are simply choosing to do something for his benefit. I think that must be what Jesus meant.

"Certainly we do not have warm feelings for people who hate us. That would be abnormal, but we can do loving acts for them. That is simply a choice. We hope that such loving acts will have a positive effect upon their attitudes and behavior and treatment, but at least we have chosen to do something positive for them."

My answer seemed to satisfy Ann, at least for the moment. I had the feeling that we would discuss that again. I also had the feeling that if the experiment was going to get off the ground, it would be because of Ann's deep faith in God.

"After the first month," I said, "I want you to ask Glenn for feedback on how you are doing. Using your own words, ask him, 'Glenn, you remember a few weeks ago when I told you I was going to try to be a better wife? I want to ask how you think I am doing.'

"Whatever Glenn says, accept it as information. Whatever his response, do not argue but accept it and assure him that you are serious about being a better wife, and if he has additional suggestions, you are open to them.

"Follow this pattern of asking for feedback once a month for the entire six months. Whenever Glenn gives you the first positive response, you will know that your efforts are getting through to him emotionally. One week after you receive the first positive feedback, I want you to make a request of Glenn—something that you would like him to do, something in keeping with your primary love language. For example, you may say to him one evening, 'Glenn, do you know something I would like to do? Do you remember how we used to go take walks in Reynolda Gardens together? I'd like to go do that with you on Thursday night. The kids are going to be staying at my mom's. Do you think that would be possible?'

"Make the request something specific, not general. Don't say, 'You know, I wish we would spend more time together.' That's too vague. How will you know when he's done it? But if you make your request specific, he will know exactly what you want and you will know that, when he does it, he is choosing to do something for your benefit.

"Do this each month. If he does it, fine; if he doesn't do it, fine. But when he does it, you will know that he is responding to your needs. In the process, you are teaching him your primary love language because the requests you make are in keeping with your love language. If he chooses to begin loving you in your primary language, your positive emotions toward him will begin to resurface. Your emotional tank will begin to fill up and in time the marriage will, in fact, be reborn."

"Dr. Chapman, I would do anything if that could happen," Ann said.

"Well," I responded, "it will take a lot of hard work, but I believe it's worth a try. I'm personally interested to see if this experiment works and if our hypothesis is true. I would like to meet with you regularly throughout this process—perhaps every two weeks—and I would like you to keep records on the positive words of affirmation that you give Glenn each week. Also, I would like you to bring me your list of complaints that you have written in your notebook without stating them to Glenn. Perhaps from the felt complaints, I can help you build specific requests for Glenn that will help meet some of those frustrations. Eventually, I want you to learn how to share your frustrations and irritations in a constructive way, and I want you and Glenn to learn how to work through those irritations and conflicts. But during this six-month experiment, I want you to write them down without telling Glenn."

Ann left, and I believed that she had the answer to her question: "Is it possible to love someone whom you hate?"

In the next six months, Ann saw a tremendous change in Glenn's attitude and treatment of her. The first month, he treated the whole thing lightly. But after the second month, he gave her positive feedback about her efforts. In the last four months, he responded positively to almost all of her requests, and her feelings for him began to change drastically. Glenn never came for counseling, but he did listen to some of my CDs and discussed them with Ann. He encouraged Ann to continue her counseling, which she did for another three months after our experiment. To this day, Glenn swears to his friends that I am a miracle worker. I know in fact that love is a miracle worker.

Perhaps you need a miracle in your own marriage. Why not try Ann's experiment? Tell your spouse that you have been thinking about your marriage and have decided that you would like to do a better job of meeting his/her needs. Ask for suggestions on how you could improve. His suggestions will be a clue to his primary love language. If he makes no suggestions, guess his love language based on the things he has complained about over the years. Then, for six months, focus your attention on that love language. At the end of each month, ask your spouse for feedback on how you are doing and for further suggestions.

Whenever your spouse indicates that he is seeing improvement, wait one week and then make a specific request. The request should be something you really want him to do for you. If he chooses to do it, you will know that he is responding to your needs. If he does not honor your request, continue to love him. Maybe next month he will respond positively. If your spouse starts speaking your love language by responding to your requests, your positive emotions toward him will return, and in time your marriage will be reborn. I cannot guarantee the results, but scores of people whom I have counseled have experienced the miracle of love.

If your marriage is in the serious trouble discussed in this chapter, you need to begin by making a strong commitment of the will to undertake the following experiment. You risk further pain and rejection, but you also stand to regain a healthy and fulfilling marriage. Count the cost; it's worth the attempt.

1. Ask how you can be a better spouse, and regardless of the other's attitude, act on what he or she tells you. Continue to both seek more input and comply with those wishes with all your heart and will. Assure your spouse that your motives are pure.

2. When you receive positive feedback, you know there is progress. Each month make one nonthreatening but specific request that is easy for your spouse. Make sure it relates to your primary love language and will help replenish your empty tank.

3. When your spouse responds and meets your need, you will be able to react with not only your will but your emotions as well. Without overreacting, continue positive feedback and affirmation of your spouse at these times.

4. As your marriage begins to truly heal and grow deeper, make sure you don't "rest on your laurels" and forget your spouse's love language and daily needs. You're on the road to your dreams, so stay there! Put appointments into your schedule to assess together how you're doing.

THE 5 love LANGUAGES®

13

A Personal Word

Well, what do you think? Having read these pages, walked in and out of the lives of several couples, visited small villages and large cities, sat with me in the counseling office, and talked with people in restaurants, what do you think? Could these concepts radically alter the emotional climate of your marriage? What would happen if you discovered the primary love language of your spouse and chose to speak it consistently?

Neither you nor I can answer that question until you have tried it. I know that many couples who have heard this concept at my marriage seminars say that choosing to love and expressing it in the primary love language of their spouse has made a drastic difference in their marriage. When the emotional need for love is met, it creates a climate where the couple can deal with the rest of life in a much more productive manner. Consider Mark and Robin. Robin figured out that Mark's primary love language was affirming words, usually involving something specific ("I like how you're protective of me; it makes me feel loved"). "It greatly helps me understand him," she said. "Now, that's not to imply that I always say the right thing! But simply knowing how he's wired has drawn us closer." Robin says her love language is acts of service. "Mark would compliment me about something, because that's his love language, and somehow it never made me feel all that great. But when we figured out that what I really valued were acts of service, even something small like bringing me coffee in bed in the morning, our marriage took a giant step."

We each come to marriage with a different personality and history. We bring emotional baggage into our marriage relationship. We come with different expectations, different ways of approaching things, and different opinions about what matters in life. In a healthy marriage, that variety of perspectives must be processed. We need not agree on everything, but we must find a way to handle our differences so that they do not become divisive. With empty love tanks, couples tend to argue and withdraw, and some may tend to be violent verbally or physically in their arguments. But when the love tank is full, we create a climate of friendliness, a climate that seeks to understand, that is willing to allow differences and to negotiate problems. I am convinced that no single area of marriage affects the rest of marriage as much as meeting the emotional need for love.

> **I dream of a day when the potential of the married couples in this country can be unleashed for the good of humankind.**

The ability to love, especially when your spouse is not loving you, may seem impossible for some. Such love may require us to draw upon our spiritual resources. A number of years ago, as I faced my own marital struggles, I rediscovered my need for God. As an anthropologist, I had been trained to examine data. I decided to personally excavate the roots of the Christian faith. Examining the historical accounts of Christ's birth, life, death, and resurrection, I came to view His death as an expression of love and His resurrection as profound evidence of His power. I became a true "believer." I committed my life to Him and have found that He provides the inner spiritual energy to love, even when love is not reciprocated. I would encourage you to make your own investigation of the One who, as He died, prayed for those who killed Him: "Father, forgive them for they know not what they do." That is love's ultimate expression.

The high divorce rate in our country bears witness that thousands of married couples have been living with an empty emotional love tank. I believe that the concepts in this book could make a significant impact upon the marriages and families of our country.

I have not written this book as an academic treatise to be stored in the libraries of colleges and universities, although I hope that professors of sociology and psychology will find it helpful in courses on marriage and family life. I have written not to those who are studying marriage but to those who are married, to those who have experienced the "in-love" euphoria, who entered marriage with lofty dreams of making each other supremely happy but in the reality of day-to-day life are in danger of losing that dream entirely. It is my hope that thousands of those couples will not only rediscover their dream but will see the path to making their dreams come true.

I dream of a day when the potential of the married couples in this country can be unleashed for the good of humankind, when husbands and wives can live life with full emotional love tanks and reach out to accomplish their potential as individuals and as couples. I dream of a day when children can grow up in homes filled with love and security, where children's developing energies can be channeled to learning and serving rather than seeking the love they did not receive at home. It is my desire that this brief volume will kindle the flame of love in your marriage and in the marriages of thousands of other couples like you.

    I wrote this for you. I hope it changes your life. And if it does, be sure to give it to someone else. I would be pleased if you would give a copy of this book to your family, to your brothers and sisters, to your married children, to your employees, to those in your civic club or church or synagogue. Who knows? Together we may see our dream come true.

For a free online study guide, please visit:

5lovelanguages.com

This group discussion guide is designed to both help couples apply the concepts from *The 5 Love Languages* and stimulate genuine dialogue among study groups.

THE 5 *love* LANGUAGES

Frequently Asked Questions

1. What if I can't discover my primary love language?

"I've taken The 5 Love Languages Profile and my scores come out almost even except for Receiving Gifts. I know that's not my primary love language. What should I do?"

In the book, I discuss three approaches to discovering your love language.

- First, observe how you most often express love to others. If you're regularly doing Acts of Service for others, this may be your love language. If you're consistently verbally affirming people, then Words of Affirmation is likely your love language.

- Second, consider what you complain about most often. When you say to your wife, "I don't think you'd ever touch me if I didn't initiate it," you're revealing that Physical Touch is your primary love language. When your wife goes on a shopping trip in the city and you say, "You didn't bring me anything?" you're indicating that Receiving Gifts is your love language. The statement "We don't ever spend time together" indicates the love language of Quality Time. Your complaints reveal your inner desires. (If you have difficulty remembering what you complain about most often, ask your wife. She'll know.)

- Third, think of the requests you make of your wife most often. If you're saying, "Will you give me a back rub?" you are asking for Physical Touch. "Do you think we could get a weekend away this month?" is a request for Quality Time. "Would it be possible for you to clean out your closet this afternoon?" expresses your desire for Acts of Service.

One husband told me that he discovered his love language by simply following the process of elimination. He knew that Receiving Gifts was not his language, so that left only four. He asked himself, "If I had to give up one of the four, which one would I give up first?" His answer was Quality Time. "Of the three remaining, if I had to give up another, which one would I give up?" He concluded that apart from sexual intercourse, he could give up Physical Touch. He could get along without the pats and hugs and holding hands. That left Acts of Service and Words of Affirmation. While he appreciated the things his wife did for him, he knew that her affirming words were really what gave him life. He could live for a whole day on one positive comment from her. That's how much they meant to him. It was no stretch to conclude that Words of Affirmation was his primary love language and Acts of Service was his secondary love language.

2. What if I can't discover my wife's love language?

"My wife hasn't read the book, but we have discussed the love languages. She says she doesn't know what her love language is."

My first suggestion is to give your wife a copy of *The 5 Love Languages: The Secret to Love That Lasts*. If she reads it, she'll likely be eager to share her love language with you. However, if she doesn't have the time or interest to read the book, I would suggest you answer variations of the three questions discussed in question #1.

- How does your wife most often express love to others?
- What does she complain about most often?
- What does she request most often?

Though your wife's complaints may sometimes irritate you, they're actually giving you valuable information. If your wife says, "We don't ever spend any time together," you may be tempted to say, "What do you mean? We went out to dinner Thursday night." Such a defensive statement will end the conversation. If, on the other hand, you respond, "What would you like for us to do?" you'll likely get a helpful answer. Your wife's complaints are the most powerful indicators of her primary love language.

Another approach is to do a five-week experiment. The first week, you focus on one of the five love languages and try to speak it every day. Observe your wife's response. On Saturday and Sunday, you relax. The second week—Monday through Friday—you focus on another of the love languages. Continue with a different language each of the five weeks. On the week you speak your wife's primary love language, you'll likely see a difference in her countenance and the way she responds to you. It will be obvious that this is her primary love language.

3. **Does your primary love language change as you get older?**
I think our primary love language tends to stay with us for a lifetime. It's like many other personality traits that develop early and remain consistent. For example, a highly organized person was likely organized as a child. A person who is laid-back and relaxed likely had those traits as a child. This is true of numerous personality traits.

However, there are certain situations in life that make the other love languages extremely attractive. For example, your primary love language may be Words of Affirmation, but if you're working two jobs, then Acts of Service by your wife may become extremely attractive to you. If she gives you only Words of Affirmation and doesn't offer to help you with household responsibilities, you may begin to think, "I'm tired of hearing you say 'I love you' when you never lift a hand to help me." For the time you're working two jobs, it may seem as though Acts of Service has become your primary love language. However, if your wife's Words of Affirmation stopped, you'd quickly realize that it was still your primary love language.

If you experience the death of a parent or a close friend, an extended hug by your wife may be the most meaningful thing for you at the moment—even if Physical Touch isn't your primary love language. There's something about being held in the midst of our grief that communicates that we're loved. So while Physical Touch isn't your primary love language, it can be very meaningful on certain occasions.

4. Does the five love language concept work with children?

Most definitely. Inside every child there's an emotional love tank. If children feel loved by their parents, they will grow up normally. But if their love tanks are empty, they will grow up with many internal struggles. During the teenage years they'll likely go looking for love, often in the wrong places. For that reason, it's extremely important that parents learn how to love children effectively. Some time ago, I teamed up with psychiatrist Ross Campbell to write *The 5 Love Languages of Children*. The book is written for parents and is designed to help them discover their child's primary love language. It also discusses how that love language interfaces with the child's anger, the child's learning, and the child's discipline.

One of the points we make in the book is that children need to learn how to receive and give love in all five languages. This produces an emotionally healthy adult. Thus, parents are encouraged to give heavy doses of the child's primary love language, then sprinkle in the other four regularly. When children receive love in all five languages, they will eventually learn how to give love in all five languages.

5. Do children's love languages change when they get to be teenagers?

A parent said, "I've read *The 5 Love Languages of Children*, and it really helped us in raising our children. However, now our son has become a teenager. We're doing the same things we've always done, but it doesn't seem to be working. I'm wondering if his love language has changed."

I don't believe a child's love language changes at age thirteen.

However, you must learn new ways to speak the child's primary love language. Whatever you've been doing in the past, the teenager considers it childish and wants nothing to do with it.

If the teen's love language is Physical Touch and you've been hugging him and kissing him on the cheek, he may well push you away and say, "Leave me alone." It doesn't mean that he doesn't need Physical Touch; it means that he considers those particular touches to be childish. You must now speak Physical Touch in more adult dialects, such as an elbow to the side, a fist to the shoulder, or a pat on the back. Or you might wrestle your teen to the floor. These touches will communicate your love to a teenager. The worst thing you can do to a teenager whose love language is Physical Touch is to withdraw when the teen says, "Don't touch me."

For more on relating to teens, see *The 5 Love Languages of Teenagers.*

6. What if the primary love language of your wife is difficult for you?

"I didn't grow up in a touching family, and now I've discovered that my wife's love language is Physical Touch. It's really difficult for me to initiate it."

The good news is that all five love languages can be learned. It's true that most of us grew up speaking only one or two of these love languages. These will come natural for us and will be relatively easy to speak. The others must be learned. As in all learning situations, small steps make for big gains.

If Physical Touch is your wife's language and you're not by nature a "toucher," begin with small things such as putting your hand on her shoulder as you pour a cup of coffee or give her a "love pat" on the shoulder as you walk by. These small touches will begin to break down the barrier. Each time you touch, the next touch will be easier. You can become proficient in speaking the language of Physical Touch.

The same is true with the other languages. If you're not a Words of Affirmation person and you discover that your wife's language is Words of Affirmation, make a list of statements that you hear from other people or that you read or hear in the media. Stand in front of a mirror and read the list until you become comfortable hearing yourself say those words. Then choose one of the statements to say to your wife. Each time you affirm her, it will become easier. Not only will your wife feel good about your changed behavior but you'll also feel good about yourself, because you'll know that you're effectively expressing love to her.

7. Are some of the love languages found more among women and others found more among men?

I've never done the research to discover if certain love languages are gender-slanted. Anecdotal evidence suggests that more men have Physical Touch and Words of Affirmation as their love language and more women have Quality Time and Receiving Gifts. But I don't know if that's statistically accurate.

I prefer to deal with the love languages as being gender-neutral. I do know that any one of the five love languages can be the primary love language of a man or the primary love language of a woman. The important thing in marriage is that you discover the primary and secondary love languages of your spouse and speak them regularly. If you do that, you will create a healthy emotional climate for marital growth.

8. **How did you discover the five love languages?**

    For years, I helped couples in the counseling office discover what their spouse desired in order to feel loved. Over time, I began to see a pattern in their responses. I discovered that what makes one person feel loved does not necessarily make another person feel loved. I read over the notes I'd made and asked myself this question: "When someone sat in my office and said, 'I feel like my spouse doesn't love me,' what did that person want?" The answers fell into five categories. I later called them the five love languages.

    I started sharing these languages in workshops and study groups. When I did, I saw the lights come on for couples who suddenly realized why they had been missing each other emotionally. When they discovered and spoke each other's primary love language, it radically changed the emotional climate of their marriage.

    I decided to write a book in which I would share the concept, hoping to influence other couples whom I would never have an opportunity to meet in person. Now that the book has sold over ten million copies in English and has been translated into fifty languages around the world, my efforts have been more than rewarded.

9. **Do the love languages work in other cultures?**

    Since my academic background is anthropology, this was my question when a Spanish publisher first requested permission to translate and publish the book in Spanish. I initially said, "I don't know if this concept works in Spanish. I discovered it in an Anglo setting."

The publisher said, "We've read the book, and it works in Spanish." Then came the French edition, the German, the Dutch, and many more. In almost every culture, the book has become a bestseller of the publisher. This leads me to believe that these five fundamental ways of expressing love are universal.

However, the *dialects* in which these languages are spoken will differ from culture to culture. For example, the kinds of touches that are appropriate in one culture may not be appropriate in another. The Acts of Service that are spoken in one culture may not be spoken in another. But when these cultural adaptations are made, the concept of the five love languages will have a profound impact on the couples in that culture.

10. Why do you think *The 5 Love Languages* has been so successful?

I believe that our deepest emotional need is the need to feel loved. If we're married, the person we would most like to love us is our spouse. If we feel loved by our spouse, the whole world is bright and life is wonderful. On the other hand, if we feel rejected or ignored, the world begins to look dark.

Most couples get married when they still have the euphoric feelings of being "in love." When the euphoric feelings evaporate sometime after the wedding and the couple's differences begin to emerge, they often find themselves in conflict. With no positive plan for resolving conflicts, they resort to speaking harshly to each other. Harsh words create feelings of hurt, disappointment, and anger. Not only do the husband and wife feel unloved but they also begin to resent each other.

When couples read *The 5 Love Languages*, they discover why they lost the romantic feelings of courtship and how emotional love can be rekindled in their relationship. Once they begin speaking each other's primary love language, they are surprised to see how quickly their emotions turn positive. With a full love tank, they can process their conflicts in a much more positive manner and find solutions that are workable.

The rebirth of emotional love creates a positive emotional climate between them, and they learn to work together as a team—encouraging, supporting, and helping each other reach meaningful goals.

Once this happens, they want to share the message of the five love languages with all their friends. I believe the success of *The 5 Love Languages* can be attributed to the couples who have read it, learned to speak each other's language, and recommended it to their friends.

11. What if I speak my wife's love language and she doesn't respond?

"My wife wouldn't read the book, so I decided to speak her love language and see what would happen. Nothing happened. She didn't even acknowledge that I was doing anything differently. How long am I supposed to continue speaking her love language when there's no response?"

I know that it can become discouraging when you feel that you're investing in your marriage and receiving nothing in return. There are two possibilities as to why your wife is not responding. First, and most likely, you're speaking the wrong love language.

Many husbands assume that their wife's love language is Acts of Service. So they start tackling projects around the house. They check off items on the household to-do list at a furious pace. They are sincerely trying to speak their wife's love language. When she doesn't even acknowledge the efforts, her husband may become discouraged.

In reality, her primary love language may be Words of Affirmation. Because her husband feels no love coming from her, he may be verbally critical of her. His critical words are like daggers to her heart, so she withdraws from him. She suffers in silence while he becomes frustrated that his efforts for improving the marriage are unsuccessful. The problem is not his sincerity; the problem is that he's actually speaking the wrong love language.

On the other hand, assuming you are speaking your wife's primary love language, there is another reason why she may not be responding positively. If she is already involved in another romantic relationship, either emotionally or sexually, she will often reason that your efforts have come too late. She may even perceive that your efforts are temporary and insincere and that you're simply trying to manipulate her to stay in the marriage. Even if your wife isn't involved with someone else, if your relationship has been hostile for a long time, she may still perceive your efforts as being manipulative.

In this situation, the temptation is to give up, to stop speaking her love language because it's not making any difference. The worst thing you can do is to yield to this temptation. If you give up, it will confirm her conclusion that your efforts were designed to manipulate her.

The best approach you can take is to continue to speak her love language on a regular basis no matter how she treats you. Set yourself a goal of six months, nine months, or a year. Your attitude should be, *No matter what her response is, I'm going to love her in her love language over the long haul. If she walks away from me, she will walk away from someone who is loving her unconditionally.* This attitude will keep you on a positive path even when you feel discouraged.

There is nothing more powerful that you can do than to love your wife even when she's not responding positively. Whatever the ultimate response of your wife, you will have the satisfaction of knowing that you've done everything you could do to restore your marriage. If your wife eventually chooses to reciprocate your love, you will have demonstrated for yourself the power of unconditional love. And you will reap the benefits of the rebirth of mutual love.

12. Can love be reborn after sexual infidelity?

Nothing devastates marital intimacy more than sexual unfaithfulness. Sexual intercourse is a bonding experience. It unites two people in the deepest possible manner. Almost all cultures have a public wedding ceremony and a private consummation of the marriage in sexual intercourse. Sex is designed to be the unique expression of our commitment to each other for a lifetime. When this commitment is broken, it is devastating to the marriage.

However, this does not mean that the marriage is destined for divorce. If the offending party is willing to break off the extramarital involvement and do the hard work of rebuilding the marriage, there can be genuine restoration.

In my own counseling experience, I've seen scores of couples who have experienced healing after sexual infidelity. It involves not only breaking off the extramarital affair but also discovering what led to the affair in the first place.

Success in restoration is a two-pronged approach. First, the offending party must be willing to explore their own personality, beliefs, and lifestyle that led them to the affair. There must be a willingness to change attitudes and behavior patterns. Second, the couple must be willing to take an honest look at the dynamics of their marriage and be open to replacing destructive patterns with positive patterns of integrity and sincerity. Both of these solutions will normally require the help of a professional counselor.

Research indicates that the couples who are most likely to survive sexual infidelity are those couples who receive both individual counseling and marriage counseling. Understanding the five love languages and choosing to speak each other's language can help create an emotional climate in which the hard work of restoring the marriage can be successful.

13. What do you do when your wife refuses to speak your love language even though she knows it?

"We both read *The 5 Love Languages*, took the profile, and discussed our primary love languages with each other. That was two months ago. My wife knows that my love language is Words of Affirmation. Yet in two months, I have yet to hear her say anything positive. Her love language is Acts of Service. I've started doing several things she's asked me to do around the house. I think she appreciates what I'm doing, but she never tells me."

Let me begin by saying that we cannot make our spouse speak our love language. Love is a choice. We can request love, but we cannot demand it. Having said that, let me suggest some reasons why your wife may not be speaking your love language.

She may have grown up in a home where she received few positive words. Her parents were perhaps very critical of her. Thus, she did not have a positive role model when it comes to speaking Words of Affirmation. Such words may be very difficult for her to verbalize. It will require effort on her part and patience on your part as she learns to speak a language that's foreign to her.

A second reason that she may not be speaking your love language is that she fears that if she gives you Words of Affirmation for the few changes you've made, you'll become complacent and not go on to make the major changes she's hoping for. It is the mistaken idea that if I reward mediocrity, I will curtail the person's aspirations to be better. That is a commonly held myth that keeps some parents from verbally affirming children. Of course, it's untrue. If a person's primary love language is Words of Affirmation, those words challenge the person to greater levels of accomplishment.

My suggestion is that you initiate the love tank game discussed in chapter 9. You ask her, "On a scale of zero to ten, how full is your love tank?" If she answers anything less than 10, you ask, "What could I do to help fill it?" Whatever she says, do it to the best of your ability. If you do this once a week for a month, chances are she will start asking you how full your love tank is. And you can begin making requests of her. This is a fun way of teaching her how to speak your love language.

14. Can emotional love return after it's been gone for thirty years?

"We're not enemies. We don't fight. We simply live in the same house like roommates."

Allow me to answer this question with a true story. A couple came to me at one of my seminars. The husband said, "We've come to thank you for bringing new life to our marriage. We've been married for thirty years, but the last twenty years have been extremely empty. If you want to know how bad our marriage has been, we haven't taken a vacation together in twenty years. We simply live in the same house, try to be civil, and that's about it.

"A year ago, I shared my struggle with a friend. He went into his house, came back with your book *The 5 Love Languages* and said to me, 'Read this. It will help you.' The last thing I wanted to do was read another book, but I did. I went home that night and read the whole book. I finished about 3:00 a.m., and with every chapter, I realized that we had failed to speak each other's love language through the years.

"I gave the book to my wife and asked if she would read it and tell me what she thought of it. Two weeks later, she said, 'I read the book.' 'What did you think about it?' I asked. 'I think if we had read that book thirty years ago, our marriage would have been very different.' I said to her, 'That's the same thought I had. Do you think it would make any difference if we tried now?' She responded, 'We don't have anything to lose.'

"We discussed our primary love languages and agreed that we would try to speak each other's language at least once a week to see what would happen. If anyone had told me that in two months I would have love feelings for her again, I would never have believed it. But I did."

His wife spoke up and said, "If anyone had told me that I would ever have love feelings for him again, I would have said, 'No way. Too much has happened.'" She then said, "This year we took our first vacation together in twenty years and had a wonderful time. We drove four hundred miles to come to your seminar and enjoyed being with each other. I'm just sad that we wasted so many years of simply living in the same house when we could have had a love relationship. Thank you for your book."

"Thank you for sharing your story," I said. "I find it greatly encouraging. I hope you make the next twenty years so exciting that the last twenty will be a dim memory."

"That's what we intend to do," they both said together.

Can emotional love be reborn in a marriage after thirty years? Yes, if the two of you are willing to try speaking each other's love language.

15. I'm single. How does the love language concept apply to me?

Through the years, many single adults have said to me, "I know you wrote your original book for married couples. However, I read it and it helped me in all my relationships. Why don't you write a book on the five love languages for singles?" And so I did. It's entitled *The 5 Love Languages for Singles*. In the book, I try to help single adults apply the love language concept in all their relationships. I begin by helping them understand why they felt love or did not feel love growing up as a child.

One young man who is incarcerated said, "Thanks for sharing the five love languages. For the first time in my life, I finally understand that my mother loves me. I realize that my love language is Physical Touch, but my mother never hugged me. In fact, the first hug I ever remember getting from my mother was the day I left for prison. But I realize that she spoke Acts of Service very strongly. She worked hard to keep us in food and clothes and to provide a place to live. I know now that she loved me; she simply wasn't speaking my language. But now I understand she really did love me."

I also help singles apply the love language concept in their sibling relationships, work relationships, and dating relationships. I have been extremely encouraged by the response of single adults. I hope that if you're single, you'll discover what others have discovered. Expressing love in a person's primary love language enhances all relationships.

16. How do I speak my spouse's love language if he/she is away from me for a time (e.g., deployment, work, school)?

I am frequently asked how to apply the love languages in long-distance relationships. Physical touch and quality time are particularly challenging in these instances. The simple answer is this: you must be creative and committed to staying connected despite the distance.

If your love language is physical touch, then here are a few creative ideas for speaking one another's love language. First, having photographs of yourself as a couple may remind you of enjoyable times together. Having physical items that belong to one another may also remind you of each other. Perhaps a shirt or the cologne or perfume of your significant other may remind you of that person and of enjoyable times together. You also should email, text, write, etc., about how you enjoy being with one another. You might even try keeping a calendar on which you physically mark off the days until you're able to be together again. This is not a comprehensive list of ideas, but all of these are physical activities and items that will at least in part help satisfy your physical love language.

As for quality time, the time you spend staying in contact, working to encourage one another, sending each other notes and gifts, etc., is quality time. Of course, it's not the preferred form of quality time, but it is quality time nonetheless. You must learn to view it and appreciate it as such.

More specific ways you can express the language of quality time are to talk often about how you desire to stay close and keep your love alive. Read or reread *The 5 Love Languages* (or *The 5 Love Languages Military Edition*) together while you're apart, or listen to my podcasts, and discuss these together as a way of nurturing your relationship. This, too, requires commitment, but if you truly love one another, then you'll find the energy and time to stay connected.

Use your situation as an opportunity to practice the other languages as well. Notes and gifts need to be viewed as more than "just" notes and gifts. They need to be viewed as physical effort and words of affirmation meant to express love.

In closing, yes, distance is difficult in a relationship, but it does not have to be the end of the relationship. Obviously, the more time you can spend together, the better. And you should strive for this. However, if you are a committed couple and are willing to be creative in how you speak one another's love language, then your relationship can survive and even thrive during your time apart.

THE **5** *love*
LANGUAGES®

The 5 Love Languages® Profile for Couples—for Him

The 5 Love Languages Profile will give you and your spouse or significant other a thorough analysis of your emotional communication preference. It will single out your primary love language, what it means, and how you can use it to connect with your loved one with intimacy and fulfillment. Two profiles are included so that each of you can complete the assessment.

You will now see 30 paired statements. Please select the statement that best defines what is most meaningful to you in your relationship as a couple. Both statements may or may not sound like they fit your situation, but please choose the statement that captures the essence of what is most meaningful to you the majority of the time. Allow 10 to 15 minutes to complete the profile. Take it when you are relaxed, and try not to rush through it. Then tally your results and read how to interpret your profile on page 202.

It's more meaningful to me when . . .

1	I receive a loving note/text/email for no special reason from my loved one.	A
	she and I hug.	E

2	I can spend alone time with her—just the two of us.	B
	she does something practical to help me out.	D

3	she gives me a little gift as a token of our love for each other.	C
	I get to spend uninterrupted leisure time with her.	B

4	she unexpectedly does something for me like filling my car or doing the laundry.	D
	she and I touch.	E

5	she puts her arm around me when we're in public.	E
	she surprises me with a gift.	C

6	I'm around her, even if we're not really doing anything.	B
	we hold hands.	E

7	my loved one gives me a gift.	C
	I hear "I love you" from her.	A

8	I sit close to her.	E
	I am complimented by her for no apparent reason.	A

It's more meaningful to me when . . .

9
| I get the chance to just "hang out" with her. | B |
| I unexpectedly get small gifts from her. | C |

10
| I hear her tell me, "I'm proud of you." | A |
| she helps me with a task. | D |

11
| I get to do things with her. | B |
| I hear supportive words from her. | A |

12
| she does things for me instead of just talking about doing nice things. | D |
| I feel connected to her through a hug. | E |

13
| I hear praise from her. | A |
| she gives me something that shows she was really thinking about me. | C |

14
| I'm able to just be around her. | B |
| I get a back rub or massage from her. | E |

15
| she reacts positively to something I've accomplished. | A |
| she does something for me that I know she doesn't particularly enjoy. | D |

16
| she and I kiss frequently. | E |
| I sense she is showing interest in the things I care about. | B |

It's more meaningful to me when . . .

17	my loved one works on special projects with me that I have to complete.	D
	she gives me an exciting gift.	C

18	she compliments me on my appearance.	A
	she takes the time to listen to me and really understand my feelings.	B

19	we share nonsexual touch in public.	E
	she offers to run errands for me.	D

20	she does a bit more than her normal share of the responsibilities we share (around the house, work-related, etc.).	D
	I get a gift that I know she put thought into choosing.	C

21	she doesn't check her phone while we're talking.	B
	she goes out of her way to do something that relieves pressure on me.	D

22	I can look forward to a holiday because of a gift I anticipate receiving.	C
	I hear the words "I appreciate you" from her.	A

23	she brings me a little gift after she has been traveling without me.	C
	she takes care of something I'm responsible to do but I feel too stressed to do at the time.	D

It's more meaningful to me when . . .

24
| she doesn't interrupt me while I'm talking. | B |
| gift giving is an important part of our relationship. | C |

25
| she helps me out when she knows I'm already tired. | D |
| I get to go somewhere while spending time with her. | B |

26
| she and I are physically intimate. | E |
| she gives me a little gift that she picked up in the course of her normal day. | C |

27
| she says something encouraging to me. | A |
| I get to spend time in a shared activity or hobby with her. | B |

28
| she surprises me with a small token of her appreciation. | C |
| she and I touch a lot during the normal course of the day. | E |

29
| she helps me out—especially if I know she's already busy. | D |
| I hear her specifically tell me, "I appreciate you." | A |

30
| she and I embrace after we've been apart for a while. | E |
| I hear her say how much I mean to her. | A |

THE **5 love** LANGUAGES®

The 5 Love Languages® Profile for Couples—for Her

Here is the second profile. As previously mentioned, it will give you a thorough analysis of your emotional communication preference. It will single out your primary love language, what it means, and how you can use it to connect with your loved one with intimacy and fulfillment. Two profiles are included so that each of you can complete the assessment.

You will now see 30 paired statements. Please select the statement that best defines what is most meaningful to you in your relationship as a couple. Both statements may or may not sound like they fit your situation, but please choose the statement that captures the essence of what is most meaningful to you the majority of the time. Allow 10 to 15 minutes to complete the profile. Take it when you are relaxed, and try not to rush through it. Then tally your results and read how to interpret your profile on page 202.

It's more meaningful to me when...

1	I receive a loving note/text/email for no special reason from my loved one.	A
	he and I hug.	E

2	I can spend alone time with him—just the two of us.	B
	he does something practical to help me out.	D

3	he gives me a little gift as a token of our love for each other.	C
	I get to spend uninterrupted leisure time with him.	B

4	he unexpectedly does something for me like filling my car or doing the laundry.	D
	he and I touch.	E

5	he puts his arm around me when we're in public.	E
	he surprises me with a gift.	C

6	I'm around him, even if we're not really doing anything.	B
	we hold hands.	E

7	my loved one gives me a gift.	C
	I hear "I love you" from him.	A

8	I sit close to him.	E
	I am complimented by him for no apparent reason.	A

It's more meaningful to me when . . .

9
| I get the chance to just "hang out" with him. | B |
| I unexpectedly get small gifts from him. | C |

10
| I hear him tell me, "I'm proud of you." | A |
| he helps me with a task. | D |

11
| I get to do things with him. | B |
| I hear supportive words from him. | A |

12
| he does things for me instead of just talking about doing nice things. | D |
| I feel connected to him through a hug. | E |

13
| I hear praise from him. | A |
| he gives me something that shows he was really thinking about me. | C |

14
| I'm able to just be around him. | B |
| I get a back rub or massage from him. | E |

15
| he reacts positively to something I've accomplished. | A |
| he does something for me that I know he doesn't particularly enjoy. | D |

16
| he and I kiss frequently. | E |
| I sense he is showing interest in the things I care about. | B |

It's more meaningful to me when . . .

17	my loved one works on special projects with me that I have to complete.	D
	he gives me an exciting gift.	C

18	he compliments me on my appearance.	A
	he takes the time to listen to me and really understand my feelings.	B

19	we share nonsexual touch in public.	E
	he offers to run errands for me.	D

20	he does a bit more than his normal share of the responsibilities we share (around the house, work-related, etc.).	D
	I get a gift that I know he put thought into choosing.	C

21	he doesn't check his phone while we're talking.	B
	he goes out of his way to do something that relieves pressure on me.	D

22	I can look forward to a holiday because of a gift I anticipate receiving.	C
	I hear the words "I appreciate you" from him.	A

23	he brings me a little gift after he has been traveling without me.	C
	he takes care of something I'm responsible to do but I feel too stressed to do at the time.	D

It's more meaningful to me when . . .

24
he doesn't interrupt me while I'm talking.	B
gift giving is an important part of our relationship.	C

25
he helps me out when he knows I'm already tired.	D
I get to go somewhere while spending time with him.	B

26
he and I are physically intimate.	E
he gives me a little gift that he picked up in the course of his normal day.	C

27
he says something encouraging to me.	A
I get to spend time in a shared activity or hobby with him.	B

28
he surprises me with a small token of his appreciation.	C
he and I touch a lot during the normal course of the day.	E

29
he helps me out—especially if I know he's already busy.	D
I hear him specifically tell me, "I appreciate you."	A

30
he and I embrace after we've been apart for a while.	E
I hear him say how much I mean to him.	A

Look back through the letters you circled and record the number of responses in the spaces below.

A:_____ B:_____ C:_____ D:_____ E:_____

A = Words of Affirmation B = Quality Time C = Receiving Gifts
D = Acts of Service E = Physical Touch

INTERPRETING YOUR PROFILE SCORE

The highest score indicates your primary love language (the highest score is 12). It's not uncommon to have two high scores, although one language does have a slight edge for most people. That just means two languages are important to you.

The lower scores indicate those languages you seldom use to communicate love and that probably don't affect you very much on an emotional level.

IMPORTANT TO REMEMBER

You may have scored more highly on certain love languages than others, but do not dismiss those other languages as insignificant. Your loved one may express love in those ways, and it will be helpful to you to understand this about him.

In the same way, it will benefit your spouse or significant other to know *your* primary love language in order to best express affection for you in ways that you interpret as love. Every time you or he speaks each other's language, you score emotional points with each other. Of course, this isn't a game with a scorecard! The payoff of speaking each other's love language is a greater sense of connection. This translates into better communication, increased understanding, and, ultimately, improved romance.

If your spouse or significant other has not already done so, encourage him or her to take *The 5 Love Languages Profile* in this book, online 5lovelanguages.com/profile, or on *The 5 Love Languages* app (iOS or Android). Discuss your respective love languages, and use this insight to improve your relationship!

Notes

1. Proverbs 18:21.

2. Kelly Flanagan, "Why One Text Message Is More Romantic Than a Hundred Valentine Cards," *Untangled*, February 12, 2014, drkellyflanagan.com.

3. Luke 6:27–28; 31–32.

4. Luke 6:38.

STRENGTHEN YOUR RELATIONSHIPS
ONLINE

DISCOVER YOUR LOVE LANGUAGE AND MORE AT
www.5lovelanguages.com

OTHER WAYS TO CONNECT:

- /5lovelanguages
- /drgarychapman
- /drgarychapman
- /user/drgarychapman

ARE YOU ENGAGED?
PREMARITAL RESOURCE

Prologue

The Story of Your Marriage Starts Here.

EASY: A simple online resource that will teach you the tools you need to help your marriage last.

ENGAGING: Fun and challenging conversation topics from premarital counselor, teacher, and author Jeff Helton and #1 New York Times bestselling author Dr. Gary Chapman.

DYNAMIC: Intuitive interface that is easy to use on your computer, tablet, or mobile device. Take it anywhere!

SIGN UP FOR FREE AT
STARTMARRIAGEHERE.COM

OTHER BOOKS
WE THINK YOU'LL LOVE

Available wherever books are sold.